THE TRAINER'S MANUAL

HAPPY PARENTING: HAPPY KIDS

Dr. Joan D. Atwood

With Special Assistance from Amanda Geena Garha, M. S.

iUniverse

HAPPY PARENTING: HAPPY KIDS
THE TRAINER'S MANUAL

iUniverse books may be ordered through booksellers or by contacting:

iUniverse
1663 Liberty Drive
Bloomington, IN 47403
www.iuniverse.com
1-800-Authors (1-800-288-4677)

ISBN: 978-1-5320-6654-2 (sc)
ISBN: 978-1-5320-6655-9 (e)

Print information available on the last page.

iUniverse rev. date: 04/04/2019

NYMFT
New York Marriage and Family Therapists
Dr. Joan D. Atwood
With Special Assistance from Amanda Geena Garha, M. S.

Happy Parenting:
Happy Kids
The Trainer's Manual

NYMFT
New York Marriage and Family Therapists

Presents

Happy Parenting:
Happy Kids
The Trainer's Manual

Dr. Joan D. Atwood
With Special Assistance from Amanda Geena Garha, M. S.
516 764 2526
jatwood@optonline.net
http:www.NYMFT.Com

TABLE OF CONTENTS

DETAILED TABLE
OF CONTENTS

INTRODUCTION

INTRODUCTION

PHILOSOPHY

This Program supports the idea that the most challenging role in society today is that of being a parent. Yet, there are few, if any, educational programs that help parents develop the attributes necessary to meet the needs of this role. It is also apparent that traditional methods of raising children are no longer as effective as they were a generation ago. The Program model not only provides parents with realistic and practical methods for meeting the challenges of raising children today; but it also provides Professionals with a complete training course in Parent Education, leading to the Parent Educator Certification.

The Program offers a safe, supportive environment where parents become actively involved in discussing common concerns, while learning effective, enjoyable ways to relate to their children. Parents develop increased confidence and learn to maximize their potentials skills in order to create more satisfying and more productive relationships with their children.

While many specific topics are covered, for parents, the overall goal of the program is twofold:

1. To improve and enhance parent-child relationships
2. To help parents learn the skills necessary to raise responsible children who will grow into responsible adults capable of living meaningful, happy lives!

Specific Objectives for the Parenting Program

1. Parents identify, acknowledge, and use emotions to build positive relationships with their children.

2. Parents utilize emotions to improve communication and listening skills.

3. Parents examine the effects of biases, perceptions, appraisal processes, and possible self-fulfilling prophecies on parent-child relationships.

4. Parents learn to use encouragement and to be optimistic in their expectations of their children.

5. Parents increase understanding and develop realistic expectations from knowledge of children's developmental issues.

6. Parents increase awareness of the role of emotions in implementing effective discipline.

7. Parents learn various approaches to discipline to foster cooperation and avoid daily battles with their children.

8. Parents develop skills for resolving conflicts and exploring alternatives with their children.

9. Parents learn methods for developing responsibility and cooperation in their children.

10. Parents explore and develop alternative scripts to deal with both their anger and their children's anger.

11. Professionals identify topics related to parenting issues that are relevant to parenting.

12. Professionals survey parents upon completion of the program to ascertain the usefulness of the program.

Guidelines for Parents in the Parenting Program

Parents are expected to be respectful to themselves and to other parents. Therefore, we encourage all members to freely contribute to group discussions and maintain the highest level of respect when others are contributing as well. To reinforce this, we maintain the following guidelines:

- ✓ **NO CROSS-TALK**: Do not speak while others are speaking. There should not be any side conversations among other group members when another parent is sharing.

- ✓ **"I" STATEMENTS**: Parents are directed to use "I" statements when answering others in the room. Remember to talk about your **own** experience.

- ✓ **OFFER SUPPORTIVE ADVICE**: Give statements that reinforce positive growth for each other.

- ✓ **NON-JUDGMENTAL ACCEPTANCE OF OTHER PARENTS VIEWPOINTS**: Do not judge or blame others, it is important to suspend individual value judgments, and encourage one another to safely explore experiences that may not generally be accepted.

✓ **MAINTAIN CONTINUITY AND COMMITMENT**: Arrive on time and attend every session. Parents are asked to commit to all of the program's sessions and to arrive promptly so that the group can begin on time.

MODULE 1

Overview of the Program and Model

Overview of Module I

This module familiarizes the Professional with the Theoretical Assumptions of the Program. This section is discussed with clients in a very superficial way. Only generalized terminology is used.

How to Use This Program

This course is separated into twelve modules. Each module provides the Professional with information about Parent Education. In addition, it provides the Professional with the materials necessary to run a 12-session group. All forms and exercises are included within the text on separate sheets that may be copied for parents to utilize.

The program is progressive in that each module builds on the one prior. While each module stands alone, it is useful to follow the module order so that the probing and exploration into their anger response by the participant deepens as they progress.

This program teaches the Professional Educator the information necessary to see individual clients for Parent Education or to run parent groups. Please keep in mind that it is believed that a 12-session program is the tip of the iceberg. It will serve to expose parents to good parenting ideas and skills. If the parents are experiencing anger in relation to their child, it will help them get control over their anger response. It will help them become more aware of good communication skills that enhance their relationships with their children. The program is not appropriate for persons with deep-seated psychological problems. It is appropriate for persons who truly wish to learn good parenting skills so that they can have better relationships with their children.

It is recommended that after the 12-session group is completed that Parents be offered the option of continuing the group. Some of the individuals may opt for individual therapy to continue their exploration or some may wish to begin couples therapy to try to enhance their marriage or couple relationship. These options should be afforded to them or appropriate referrals given to them.

The groups are set up with 8-12 individuals in each group. This is what research shows to be the optimal number for group work. Sessions run 1 and ½ hours (90 minutes) and groups meet weekly.

The course is based on Cognitive Behavioral Psychology and Solution Focused Therapy Techniques. The course is available ONLINE (http:www.NYMFT.Com), is offered at the New York Marriage and Family Therapy offices in Rockville Centre, Williston Park, and Sag Harbor, Long Island and in New York City and can be reached by phone on (516) 764-2526. It is also available as a workshop for sports teams, school health courses, correction and parole officers, mental health clinics, court personnel, judges, attorneys, etc. For more information, please call or email jatwood@optonline.net.

The course is interactive in as much as parents have access to a facilitator after they complete the course and can submit questions and receive answers within 24 hours. The purpose of this is to assist parents with setting up and running their first group.

In addition, aside from the materials and information given on Parent Education to Professionals, they are given information on group process—the nuts and bolts of how to run a group, what to look for, how to facilitate.

THE PSYCHOLOGICAL BASIS OF THE PROGRAM

COGNITIVE BEHAVIORAL PSYCHOLOGY (CBT)

Cognitive and/or behavioral psychotherapies (CBP) are psychological approaches based on scientific principles that research has shown to be effective for a wide range of problems. Clients and therapists work together, once a therapeutic alliance has been formed, to identify and understand problems in terms of the relationship between thoughts, feelings and behavior. The approach usually focuses on difficulties in the here and now, and relies on the therapist and client developing a shared view of the individual's problem. This then leads to identification of personalized, usually time-limited therapy goals and strategies, which are continually monitored and evaluated. The treatments are inherently empowering in nature, the outcome being to focus on specific psychological and practical skills (e.g. in reflecting on and exploring the meaning attributed to events and situations and re-evaluation of those meanings) aimed at enabling clients to tackle their problems by harnessing their own resources. The acquisition and utilization of such skills is seen as the main goal, and the active component in promoting change with an emphasis on putting what has been learned into practice between sessions ("homework"). Thus the overall aim is for the individual to attribute improvement in their problems to their own efforts, in collaboration with the psychotherapist.

Cognitive psychology is a theoretical perspective that focuses on the realms of human perception, thought, and memory. It portrays learners as active processors of information--a metaphor borrowed from the computer world--and assigns critical roles to the knowledge and perspective students bring to their learning. What learners do to enrich information, in the view of cognitive psychology, determines the level of understanding they ultimately achieve.

Lev Vygotsky (1978) emphasized the role of social interactions in knowledge construction. Social constructivism turns attention to children's interactions with parents, peers, and teachers in homes, neighborhoods, and schools. Vygotsky introduced the concept of the *zone of proximal development*, which is the difference between the difficulty level of a problem a client can cope with independently and the level that can be accomplished with help from others. In the zone of proximal development, a client and a therapist work together on problems that the student alone could not work on successfully.

Cognitive and or behavioral psychotherapists work with individuals, families and groups. The approaches can be used to help anyone irrespective of ability, culture, race, gender or sexual preference.

Underlying Theory of Cognitive Therapy

The central insight of cognitive therapy as originally formulated over three decades ago is that thoughts mediate between stimuli, such as external events, and emotions. As in the figure below, a stimulus elicits a thought -- which might be an evaluative judgment of some kind -- which in turn gives rise to an emotion. In other words, it is not the stimulus *itself*, which somehow elicits an emotional response directly, but our evaluation of or thought about that stimulus. Two ancillary assumptions underpin the approach of the cognitive therapist:

- The client is capable of becoming aware of his or her own thoughts and of changing them
- Sometimes the thoughts elicited by stimuli distort or otherwise fail to reflect reality accurately

Event → Definition of the Situation → Emotion and Behavior

Some Cognitive Behavioral Therapy Principles:

Behavior is learned
All behavior is learned and just as it was learned it could be unlearned.

Reinforcement
To reinforce is anything that increases the probability that a behavior will occur. Behavior that is reinforced is likely to occur more frequently. The client defines what is reinforced.

Goals

The therapist and client set up goals for the therapy. Therapy becomes a structured situation whereby client takes action steps toward accomplishing the goals of therapy.

Shaping and Successive Approximations

The way to work toward a terminal behavior is to reinforce baby steps toward that behavior. So that anything that approximates the goal or terminal behavior is reinforced.

Thoughts Lead To Feelings

An event occurs. Based on our early childhood socialization and ongoing socialization, we define the event. Based on that definition, we experience thoughts and feelings. Based on those thoughts and feelings, we behave or act. Actions have consequences. Behaviors that have positive outcomes tend to be repeated. Behaviors that have negative outcomes tend not to be replicated.

Distorted Thoughts Lead to Negative Communication

Faulty thinking needs to be debunked and changed. There are many ways we distort our thinking. These must be worked on. There are specific techniques for changing distorted thinking.

Positive Self-Talk

Negative thinking and negative communication often gets us into trouble with ourselves or with others. Positive self-talk is a technique that could be used to change negative thinking.

Positive Action

While the therapist and client will "talk" to each other, the focus is on action. Doing things that will make you get closer to your goals and thus help you to feel better.

Contracts

Often therapist and client or client and family or client with himself or herself will design a contract that will help him or her accomplish goals.

SOLUTION FOCUSED BRIEF THERAPY

From Wikipedia, the free encyclopedia
(Redirected from Brief psychotherapy)

Solution Focused Brief Therapy can be referred to by other professionals as Solution Focused Therapy or even brief therapy, hereafter referred to as SFBT. This type of therapy utilizes a social constructionist philosophic model. Instead of focusing on what the problem is, therapists focus on what the client can obtain out of therapy. SFBT's approach minimizes focusing on previous or past problems and focuses more on what the future entails for the client. The clients are encouraged to envision what it is they want to see in the future, with therapists inviting them to explore through a curiosity approach. These changes could be small or big, but impact the clients to move towards change. Therapists ask questions to understand the client's narrative, learn about their strengths and what they consider resources, and what the exceptions to the problem described are.

For the therapist practicing with a SFBT approach, their core belief is that change is constant. When the therapist helps the client figure out what it is they want to change in their lives, as well as what they want to remain the same, the therapist will then help the client identify a concrete vision of what they want in their preferred future. The therapist will also then help the client identify in their current life what will bring them to this preferred future and how these situations could be altered or modeled in their lifestyle. When the client and therapists are able to visualize and repeat these successes, whether small or big, the client develops awareness.

The Miracle Question

The miracle question is a popular technique used by many professionals to get a better understanding of what an individual envisions in their future when they no longer see the problem in this vision. This technique is popularly used by therapists, coaches, and counselors.

An example of a miracle question would be as follows:

"Suppose that you leave today and you go about the rest of your day completing things that needed to be done. When you get into bed, exhausted, you fall into a deep sleep. Sometime, throughout the night, without you being aware, a miracle happens that solves all the problems that we have discussed and initially brought you here in the first place. But, no one knows this miracle occurred, including yourself. When you wake up the next morning, how will you know that the miracle happened... what else are you going to notice... what else?

Every client will have a different variation of the miracle question, especially since every client comes in with a different story to tell. In another situation, a counselor or therapist may ask:

"If tomorrow morning you woke up and you realized that you no longer lost your temper quickly, what would you see differently? What would the first signs be that you discovered a miracle occurred?" The same client (in this situation a child) may say "I would not get upset if someone called me names".

Scaling Questions

Another tool used by many professionals are scaling questions, which are used to identify differences for the client that can also help with goal establishment. Typically, the scales are from zero to ten, with zero to one being, the worst the problem has ever been, and ten being, the best thing that could ever happen. Clients usually choose the number based off of what question is being asked and therapists can help clients identify resources, (example - what's stopping you from slipping one point lower on the scale), as well as exceptions (example - on a day that you are one point higher on the scale, what would tell you that it was a one point higher day?) and even to describe the preferred future (example – where on the scale would be good enough? What would a day at that point on the scale look like?)

Exception Seeking Questions

SFBT also utilizes a technique called exception seeking questions. This means that there are always times when the problem could be considered less then what the problem is describing and can even be absent or less severe for a portion of the time. The counselor or therapist will probe to see if the client can describe why these situations may have been different and evaluate the different circumstances. The main goal for the client would be to mimic this behavior that has worked for them prior to, and help them gain the confidence to make their preferred future improved.

Coping Questions

When asking a client coping questions, the main objective is to understand what resources the clients have, either identified or previously unknown to them. Even when the client feels the most hopeless, there can be examples that can be taken from their narrative to help them understand what a resource can be. For example, a therapist may say, "I can see that things have gotten really difficult for you, but I can't help but be amazed by how you are able to manage to get up and do what is necessary to get your children to school. How are you able to pull this off?" When a professional is able to demonstrate this genuine curiosity and empathy, the therapist is able to highlight the client's strengths without appearing to contradict the client's view of reality. In the beginning, the therapist demonstrates summarizing, stating "I can see that things have gotten really difficult for you" so that the client feels validated. The second part of the statement, "manage to get up and do what is necessary…" is also truism, but it helps the clients see a different perspective which counters the initial narrative. Coping questions create a space for questioning to be gentle and supportive but also a way to challenge the narrative.

Resources

A key task in SFBT is to help clients identify and attend to their skills, abilities, and external resources (e.g. social networks). This process not only helps to construct a narrative of the client as a competent individual, but also aims to help the client identify new ways of bringing these resources to bear upon the problem. Resources can be identified through scaling questions, problem-free talk, or during exception-seeking.

Solution Focused Brief Therapy has branched out in numerous spectrums. Most notably, the field of Addiction Counseling has begun to utilize SFBT as an effective means to treat problem drinking. The Center for Solutions in Cando, ND has implemented SFBT is part of their program, wherein they utilize this therapy as part of a partial hospitalization and residential treatment facility for both adolescents and adults.

Thus the Parent Education Program is a blend of the two approaches to therapy. The main assumptions of this approach are:

- The focus is on the here and now.
- The problem or issue-in-living the person is experiencing is learned.
- Just as it was learned, it can be unlearned.
- They have tried many ways to solve their problem—all to no avail.
- Therapy is a relationship between client and therapist.

- Client defines the goal and the therapist assists with achieving the goal.
- Therapy involves mobilizing individual's resources and strengths to seeing new solutions.
- Therapy is brief, solution focused, goal oriented, and utilizing behavioral principles.
- Regarding poor parenting, individuals do this because they have learned to behave in this manner.
- By getting to know the thoughts people tell themselves about certain situations and the meanings they give to the thoughts, they then feel a certain way. Thus, an event in the external world occurs. Individuals give that event a certain definition and meaning. These definitions and meanings then lead to the individual feeling a certain way. If the feeling is frustrated, then individuals will behave in a frustrated or angry way.
- Behavior has consequences. Anger responses have consequences—both positive and negative. The negative consequences of the anger response far outweigh the positive consequences.
- Just as individuals learned the angry response, they can unlearn it.
- Learning new skills that replace the inappropriate ones help individuals unlearn the response.
- Positive and negative. The negative consequences of the anger response far outweigh the positive consequences.
- Just as individuals learned the angry response, they can unlearn it.
- Learning new skills that replace the inappropriate ones help individuals unlearn the response.

* * *

Model of Human Behavior

At this point a model of human behavior can be presented. There is socialization from birth until death. There is early childhood socialization by our early caretakers, usually parents. There is also on-going socialization in the schools we attend, the jobs we hold. These are the inputs to how we see the world. They are constantly changing and modified. They are what give us our worldviews and our belief systems. Based on our worldview, an event happens and we define the situation. Based on how we define the situation, we experience feelings. These feelings lead us then to behave in certain ways. Behavior has consequences and the consequences of behavior feed back into our worldviews and definition of the situation.

An example of this is how our parents handle childrearing, stress and anxiety. This will influence how we then handle childrearing, stress and anxiety. Based on our early childhood socialization, we learn to define certain situation as positive or stressful and we react to that situation in varying ways (depending on how we defined them). Parents are not the only inputs to our behavior and as we mature, other influences impinge on our worldview. Maybe we will incorporate other situations as stressful or maybe there will be a decrease in the number of situations that we define as stressful. Our worldview is constantly being influenced. If the community in which we live condones hitting of children, we learn to condone it also. So if we watch a child being hit by his/her parent, we may see that as a typical situation. "Well she had it coming to her." Based on that definition, we might do nothing to help her. But say for example we move to a different culture and we get a full view of a very different manner in which children are being hit. Well then, there is another input to our behavior. Perhaps this input will be salient enough for us to alter our worldview somewhat. Perhaps we become not as accepting of children being hit. The next time we are in that situation where we witness a child being pushed or shoved, our response might be agitation. We might even act to try to stop the encounter. Our worldview was altered by incoming socialization. This altered how we defined the situation, which in turn caused us to experience certain feelings. Then we acted differently than we did the first time.

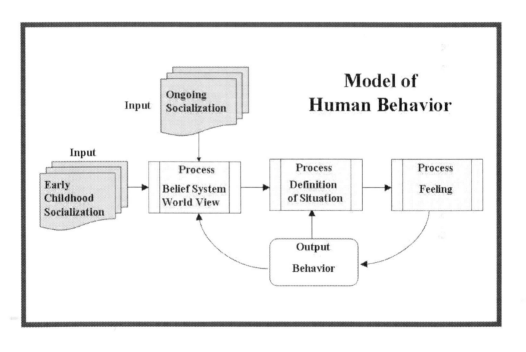

13

MODULE 2

Overview of Group Dynamics

HISTORY OF GROUP THERAPY

1900-1920: The Practical Beginnings

- **Joseph Gaither Pratt** studied how people with medical issues (Tuberculosis) fared and coped when grouped together.
- **L. Cody Marsh** developed a group treatment for a psychiatric population.
- **Edward Layzell** (1919) introduced group therapy with schizophrenics.

1920-1930- Theoretical Underpinnings

- **Gustave Le Bon** published *The Crowd*. This generated much interest in how individuals behaved in groups.
- **Sigmund Freud** published *Group Psychology and the Analysis of the Ego.*
- **Burrow** developed a program in NYC that enabled individuals to free themselves from their masks.
- **Jacob L. Moreno** introduced the name **Group Therapy.**

1930s-1945 the Age of Integration

- **Louis Wender** conducted the first psychoanalytic group in NY.
- **Samuel Richard Slavson** worked with children in groups.

- In 1943 Slavson founded **the American Group Therapy Association.**
- **Alexander Wolff** said group therapy was cost effective for those who cannot afford individual psychoanalysis.
- **Wolf and Schwartz** started the first **Group Therapy Certificate** program in New York Medical College in the late 1940s.
- **Moreno** felt psychoanalysis dwelled too much on the past and he started the **American Society Psychotherapy of Psychodrama**. He started a debate between the analysts and the more here and now focused Moreno. Moreno felt he was the **Father of Group Therapy** not Pratt and he coined the term **Group Psychotherapy.**

1945-1960 the Age of Expansion

WWI created an interest in group therapy. WWII prompted the growth of group therapy. Theorists dealt with the overflow of troops in hospitals.

- **Wilfred Bion** looked at the unconscious life of the group, using Melanie Klein's Object Relations Theory.
- **Henry Ezriel** acted Bion's unconscious life of the group but also believed the therapist must also pay attention to individual dynamics.
- **S.H. Foulkes** termed the leader of the group is the conductor who is non-authoritarian and non-directive, who attends to both group and individuals.
- **Kurt Lewin** developed a meta-theory of group life. **Lewin's Field Theory** became the basis for the T Group movement in Britain and US. The group possesses qualities that transcend those of any individuals.

1960-1970 Group Therapy Enters the Community

The Community Mental Health Act of 1963 prompted the widespread use of the group.

- **Carl Rogers** devised the basic encounter group in the 1960s.

1970-1985

- **Irving Yalom** published *The Theory and Practice of Group Psychotherapy* in 1970, the bible of group therapy. He believed the purpose of the group is to enable the individual to improve his or her capacity to have positive relationships with others.

1985-Present

Managed Health Care influences all of therapy.
Addressed the following:

- Increasing cost of Mental Health Therapy
- Need for short term mental health care
- Need for clear treatment plans
- Need for more collaborative model between different types of practitioners
- Increasing importance of the professional organizations in the field,
- An increasing attention to ethical and legal rights
- The focus on addressing multiculturalism and diversity

Five Stages of Group Development

Successful groups move through five phases throughout their lifetime. Tuckman identifies five stages of development and calls them: Forming, Storming, Norming, Performing, Adjourning.

Other researchers have labeled similar stages of group development. Charrier (1974) calls them Polite or why we're Here, Bid for Power, Constructive, and Esprit. Cooke and Widdis (1988) call them Polite or Purpose, Power, Positive, and Proficient.

> Jones (1974) depicts the model to show the four typical stages in the evolution of a group in relation to two major dimensions of personal relations and task functions.

The personal relations dimension of the model encompasses all the interrelationships that people develop and sustain in the group – their feelings, expectations, commitments, assumptions, and problems with one another. The stages of personal relations correlate with the development of the identity and functions of a group from the personal orientations of individual members. The stages of task functions correlate with the progress of a group in understanding and accomplishing its work. As a group moves through the personal relations and task functions stages simultaneously, the progress and setbacks in one dimension influence the behavior and progress in the other.

Task Functions

The stages of group development are sequential and developmental. A group will proceed through these five stages only as far as its members are willing to grow. Group cohesiveness seems to depend on how well group members can relate in the same phase at the same time. Each member must be prepared to give up something at each step in order to make the group move to the next stage. The timing of each will depend on the nature of the group, the members, and the leadership of the group. Issues and concerns must be resolved in each stage before the group can move on. If the group is not able to resolve such issues, the dominant behavior will become either apathy or conflict, and group disintegration will result.

Stage 1: Forming

When you are in the stage for forming or formation, your personal relationships are categorized as dependent. The members are the groups need a safe environment, and therefore find themselves dependent on group leaders for guidance and direction. Members of the groups have a desire for acceptance by the group and a need to be sure that the group is safe. They want to avoid conflict. Serious issues and feelings are avoided, and people focus on being busy with routines, such as when they will meet, etc. They set about gathering impressions and data about the similarities and differences among them and forming preferences for future sub-grouping. Rules of behavior seem to be to keep things simple and avoid controversy. Serious topics and feelings are avoided. This is a comfortable stage to be in but nothing much is getting done.

The major task functions also concern orientation. Members attempt to become oriented to the task as well as to one another. Discussion centers around defining the scope of the task, how to approach it, and similar concerns.

To grow from this stage to the next, each member must relinquish the comfort of non-threatening topics and risk the possibility of conflict.

This is the stage of joining, welcoming, building relationships.

If the purpose or membership seems exclusive, or people don't feel welcomed, they might not join or might be tentative or suspicious.

Appropriate Leadership Style

Since groups in this phase require definitions of their roles and goals they will need information from the leader about the group's agenda, deadlines, etc. The leader should provide as much structure as possible and become the emotional center of the team.

Specific Leader Actions

You should listen carefully, be visible, maintain open communication/ feedback channels for the team, offer support and reassurance, keep group members accountable for day-to-day results, and create team traditions.

Specific Group Member Responsibilities

Group members can help the team building process by accepting the new team identity, by learning the group's mission, and by getting to know one another.

Stage 2: Storming

In group settings, conflict is inevitable in personal relationships of group members, particularly since everyone organizes, has different feelings, ideas, attitude and beliefs. Because of fear of exposure or weakness and even failing at tasks, individuals may want a concrete structure or clarification and commitment to this structure placed. Although these conflicts may or may not be vocalized, these issues do exists. Delegating roles, such as who will be responsible for what part, what the guidelines and how to evaluate, as well as who leadership will be, how structure is set, who has what power will reflect in conflicts.

Some members may become more vocal then others who remain silent. This may be because of the discomfort created at this stage, and there may be an imminent shift in behaviors based on emerging issues of competition and hostility.

To combat these kinds of conflicts and move to the next stage, creating a testing and proving mentality to a problem solving mentality is crucial. To do so, the most important trait in helping these groups is to listen to them.

This is the stage of setting expectations, establishing styles, learning leadership and member roles, establishing processes and establishing goals.

If expectations are not clear, people may not meet them.

If expectations are not met, frustrations may arise.

If judgments arise about styles and roles, people may act critically.

If oppressive behavior happens and or is condoned, people may be hurt or want apologies or even want to quit.

If the group's goals don't match the members' goals, members may be frustrated.

At this stage leaders should be stating expectations. Individual confrontations may be happening and listening should be taking place. Group discussions are now starting.

Appropriate Leadership Style

Groups in this stage still require a high level of directive supervision, but also need considerable support. The leader must not only serve as mediator, but also as a teacher of group norms and values. The leader also needs to listen to group problems, manage conflicts, encourage participation, provide recognition, and build alliances.

Specific Leader Actions

You need to stay approachable; provide answers, answers, and more answers; repeat key information often; set short-term goals; restate mission, objectives, and priorities; and create opportunities for participation.

Specific Group Member Responsibilities

Group members must focus on the commonalties of the group and not the differences.

Stage 3: Norming

According to Tuckman's norming stage, cohesion is defined by interpersonal relations. Acknowledging who contributed what, community building and maintenance and solving issues that arise are all necessary to change preconceived notions or opinions. These can be addressed by other group members and this allows for active participation by allowing group members to question each other. This also allows for leadership to be a shared activity, and addresses to dissolve the formation of cliques. Trust and personal relations are created by allowing each other to develop personal relationships. During this stage, group cohesion is created which creates a sense of catharsis at having resolved interpersonal conflicts.

The major task function of stage three is the data flow between group members; they share feelings and ideas, solicit and give feedback to one another, and explore actions related to the task. Creativity is high. If this stage of data flow and cohesion is attained by the group members, their interactions are characterized by openness and sharing of information on both a personal and task level. They feel good about being part of an effective group.

The major drawback of the Norming stage is that members may begin to fear the inevitable future break-up of the group; they may resist change of any sort.

At this stage members will air dissatisfactions. They will start to find ways through conflict. They will assess leadership. And they will assess the member's role.

If people attack the leader or organization, the leader may be defensive and may not lead well.

If the leader doesn't deal with the conflict in the manner members want, members may feel distrust and May judge the leader.

A support the leader exercise, individual discussions and group discussions should be occurring.

Appropriate Leadership Style

Groups in this stage understand the goals and tasks more thoroughly and are willing to work hard to achieve these goals. The leader should work to make the members less dependent on his/her own leadership, but still focus on providing the support people need to mesh their activities productively.

Specific Leader Actions

You must continue to keep members focused and communication channels open, solicit participation, and encourage creative thinking. Be prepared to translate organizational goals into team goals.

Specific Group Member Responsibilities

At this point group members need to master the team skills and become interdependent by removing the leader from the center of everything.

Stage 4: Performing

Not all groups will reach stage four, which is the performing stage. If group members do find themselves at this stage, they are able to demonstrate true interdependence because of the expansion of their capacity, range and depth of personal relations. During this stage, individuals are able to function as a single unit, in smaller groups are as a whole unit with equal facility. Based on the group's needs, roles and leadership may vary. This stage is marked by interdependence in personal relations and problem solving in the realm of task functions. Productivity will be demonstrated in the highest capacity, and individuals rely on self-assurance instead of group approval. Task orientation and unity is demonstrated; group identity is complete, group moral is high, and group loyalty is intense. The groups focus on problem solving, create solutions and optimum group development. Groups will try to solve problems through experimenting and focus on achievement.

Here the group is functioning well and the group sees conflict as opportunity.

If there are unresolved issues, they will keep resurfacing in another form until resolved.

If member performance isn't supported, members may burn out or attack leadership.

If leadership isn't supported, leaders may burn out, not appreciate members, and not cultivate new leaders.

Group discussions are occurring and appreciations for members and leaders is occurring.

Appropriate Leadership Style

Groups in this phase have worked through their adjustments and have become energized by the prospect of achievement. The leader can serve as ambassador/philosopher and take a less active role by allowing the group members to run the day-to-day business of the group.

Specific Leader Actions

You need to provide resources, remove obstacles, reward high performance, stimulate interaction, emphasize teamwork, and celebrate successes.

Specific Group Member Responsibilities

Group members can help by taking on more of the team's business and letting the team leader operate at the boundaries of the team.

Stage 5: Adjourning

In Tuckman's final stage, adjourning, groups will work on terminating task behaviors and disengagement from relationships. Concluding involves recognizing participation and what was achieved through these groups. Members of the group also have the opportunity to have their own personal goodbyes. What is also demonstrated by group members is apprehension, in effect – a minor crisis. For some, the termination of the group can be a regressive moment from giving up control to give up inclusion to the group. Interventions associated with the stage can be task termination and the disengagement process.

The Concept of Development

Here it is important to put closure on tasks, put closure on relationships and prepare for the next group.

If people have unspoken feelings about closure, they may procrastinate or otherwise sabotage projects.

Leadership Style in this Model Moves From:

- **Directing**
- **Coaching**
- **Motivating**
- **Mentoring**

Applications of the Model

Facilitators must be sensitive to the needs of group members in various stages of group development. By referring to this model, a facilitator can gain some insight into the inevitable stages through which a group must pass before attaining the benefits of stage four. This insight is useful both in planning group-learning situations and for monitoring a group's progress while it is in session.

As a tool to facilitate group communication and development, the model is most effective at stage three of a group's development. At this point, the members have experienced stages one and two and are in a receptive mode to internalize the implications of stage four. The model provides them with a goal they can visualize and work toward.

Paying earnest attention to strategies for reaching stage four can facilitate the movement to that stage.

If the concepts of the model are presented when a group is in stage one, they may fall on deaf ears, receiving only polite attention. If presented in stage two, the concepts become food for conflicts or are ground into oblivion by the process of organization. At stage four, the model is unnecessary.

SPECIFIC GUIDELINES AND SUGGESTIONS FOR RUNNING GROUPS

SECTION I: Getting Ready for Group

- **Pre-group Considerations**
  - Leader should be qualified and experienced in running groups
  - What will leader's main functions be?
  - What will be the main goals of the group?
  - Where will group be held? How long will it last?
  - Is your group accessible to physically handicapped?
  - Is group sensitive to members of diversity?
  - Are your sessions set up?
  - What evaluation procedures will you use to determine the degree to which the group has met its goals?
  - What follow-up procedures will you use to help members of the group integrate what they have learned?
  - Have you a procedure for screening members?
  - Some guideline questions are:
    o Why do you want to join the group?
    o Have you ever participated in a group before?
    o Do you understand the purposes and nature of the group?
    o Do you have any fears about joining the group?
    o How ready are you to take a critical look at yourself and address your anger issues?
    o What are some specific personal concerns you would like to explore?
    o What would you most hope to get from the group?
    o What would you like to know about me?

- **Preparing Parents of Minors**
  - Get written permission from parents or legal guardians before allowing members to participate in group. Make sure you know your state's requirements.

- You can invite parents and their children and/or teens to discuss their questions or concerns. Sending letters and holding a meeting with parents can prevent many problems from arising later on.

- **Preparing Teenagers and Adults**
  - With teenagers, a letter should be sent to the parents requesting permission and a Meeting should be held with both the parents and the teenagers.
  - With adults, there should be a pre-group screening to determine if the individual is appropriate for the group. See screening questions above.

- **Setting Goals**
  - Members and leaders need to set goals for themselves—both at the beginning of the group and the beginning of each session for maximum learning to occur. At the beginning of each session, a brief questionnaire can be given asking members to rate how well they are coping with the group; how well they are managing their stress; and if they feel they are making progress. The members can tell one another about their specific goals.

- **Preparing Contracts**
  - Here members write out specific behaviors that they would like to change and what they are willing to do outside of group to make these changes. Contracting is a useful method to use with psycho-educational groups. The leader and other members can say if they think the members' goals are realistic.

- **Guidelines for Designing Effective Contracts**
  - Below are some guidelines for designing effective contracts:
    - Keep the language concise and simple
    - State the goals in behavioral terms.

- Strive for realistic and obtainable goals.
- Identify short and long term goals.
- Relate personal goals to the general goals and purpose of the group.

- **Reading**
  - Reading can be a good asset for psycho-educational and therapy groups.
  - Reading can be used as a focusing technique. Themes may emerge in a group and assigning reading around that theme is helpful. Taming Your Gremlin is one such assigned book.

- **Writing Journals**
  - Members can spend 10 minutes each day recording their feelings, situations, behaviors, and ideas for courses of action. Journaling provides continuity between sessions and it also helps members use session time more efficiently.
  - Some relevant questions group members can look at in-between sessions are:
    - What is it like to be in the group?
    - How do I define the people in the group? How do I see myself in the group?
    - How do I sabotage myself in the group?
    - How can I challenge myself in the group?
    - How do I avoid sharing information in the group?
    - What is happening in the group when I am comfortable in sharing?
  - Members could also write down their reactions to the group and 10 minutes before the end of each session, members can share those feelings.

- **Letter Writing**
  - Here members can write a letter to the most important person in their life. This could be a letter of apology, a letter of love. The only stipulation is that it ends on a positive

note. The letter does not need to be given to the person it was written for or the member may decide to share it.

- **Giving Specific Questions**
  - Group leaders can design questions ahead of time that then are given to the group to ponder. In an adolescent group, the leader may ask:
    - How important to you is being accepted by the peer group?
    - How fearful are you of relating to members of the same sex? Of the opposite sex?
    - How much pressure do you feel to decide on a career?

- **Structured Questionnaires**
  - Here the leader may decide to put all the questions together in a questionnaire. Sentence Completion questionnaires are very helpful.
    - What I want most from this group is____.
    - Thinking about being in this group for the next 12 weeks, I ____.
    - One personal concern I would hope to bring up is ____.
    - Something I particularly like about myself is ____.

- **Setting up a Problem Checklist**
  - Setting up a problem checklist is another way of helping members decide how they want to use group time. Or a teenage group, develop a list of problems teenagers typically experience and ask them to write down a rating in terms of how they experience each item.

- **Using Imagination**
  - Imagine you are a novel.
    - What is your title?
    - What are your chapter headings?
    - Do you deliver what you say you will deliver?

- Which chapters were the hardest to write?
- The easiest?
- Will people feel you delivered what you advertised?
- After people have read you cover to cover, what do you think they will think?

- **Handouts**
  - Handouts will assist members to get the most out of a group. If the group is a psycho-educational group, then giving members handouts on The Differences between Assertive and Aggressive Behavior would be helpful, as would a handout on Good Communication Techniques.

- **Preparing Leaders**
  - Get yourself ready:
  - How ready do I feel for this? Am I available to the members?
    - Do I want to do this Group?
    - How effective am I in my personal life?
    - Am I doing what I would hope the members would do with their lives?
    - Am I professionally confident?
    - Do I believe in the process of the group? Or am I doing the group merely because I was told to?

- **Getting Ready**
  - Relax before you go into the group.
  - Be aware of your thoughts and feelings as you approach a group session.
  - Try some of the exercises on yourself.
  - Spend time with your co-leader if you have one.
  - Review what you plan on doing each session and discuss this with your co-leader.
  - Devote some time to thinking about the previous session.

SECTION II: The Initial Stage

- Characteristics of the Initial Stage
  - o Physical Setting and Arrangements
  - o Privacy
  - o Comfort
  - o Seating Arrangements
- Getting Groups Started
  - o Introductions
  - o Introducing Someone Else
  - o Setting a Time Limit
  - o Using Dyads and Small Groups
- The Leader's Role
  - o Focusing Members
  - o Focusing on an Issue Outside of Group
    - ▪ Techniques to Help to Focus on Issue Outside of Group
- Creating Trust
  - o Dealing with Mistrust
  - o Some Signs that Trust is Created
  - o Some Signs that Trust is Lacking
  - o Fostering Trust
- Addressing Initial Resistance
- Starting a Session
- Ending a Session
- Member Evaluations
- Leader Evaluations

SECTION III: Transition Stage

- **Dealing with Defensive and/or Problem Behaviors**
  - ▪ **Avoid labeling members as defensive or resistant.** Attempt to be patient and strive to understand what purpose their difficult behavior is serving.
  - ▪ ***Have an external focus.***

Members in this stage frequently focus on other members and on events that are external to them. They may blame others in or out of the group to make up for their own inability to trust. A method for dealing with this is to ask the person who is doing the blaming, "Why don't you turn toward John and tell him how his behavior is affecting you?"

- ***Using impersonal and global language.***
  If the leader asks a question about how members feel about being in a parent education group, and Jim answers, "Really, I don't want to be here." He is using language that will keep focus off of himself. Leader could then refocus and say, "How do you feel about being in the group, Jim?"

Some examples:
Member: People are cautious about opening up in here.
Leader: What are you cautious about John?

- ***Asking questions of others.***
  A defense in the transition stage is members asking questions of others. This drains the energy of the group and the question should be refused to the individual.

- ***The person who is silent.***
  Leaders need to respect the silent member. The leader needs to create an environment that invites members to participate rather than force them to participate. Other members will eventually ask the member to participate. Some techniques for dealing is to form an inner group of those who are participating and have them discuss what they would like to know about those who are not participating. Or to have the silent members form an inner circle and discuss how they feel about their silence.

■ *The person who monopolizes.*
Often the member who is monopolizing is not challenged by the group. In this case, sharing your reflections and observations may be all that is necessary.

• **Exploring Common Fears**
  ■ *I'm afraid you won't like me.*
  ■ *There's someone here who bothers me.*
  ■ *I'm afraid to look at what I am really like.*
  ■ *I can't see why we have to share every feeling.*
  ■ *We seem stuck in the group.*
  ■ *I don't feel safe here.*
  ■ *I can't identify with anyone here.*

• **Leader Issues**
  In this stage leader challenges tend to emerge. It is important to deal with these challenges in an appropriate way or it may affect the group. Some of the challenges will be based in reality. Some challenges may include:
  ■ *Why do we always have to focus on the negative?*
  ■ *Your leaders aren't sharing enough of yourselves.*
  ■ *Your leaders aren't very helpful.*
  ■ *You blew it.*

SECTION IV: The Working Stage

• **Characteristics of the Working Stage:**
  In this stage, you can link members by focusing on common themes. Generally members are eager to initiate work. There is a here and now focus in this stage. Here members talk about what they current think and feel. They are also willing to have direct and focused interactions with each other. Members more readily identify their goals and concerns and they take responsibility for them. Group cohesion increases. Not all groups reach this stage.

- **Working with Emerging Themes**
  Some typical themes that might emerge during this stage are:
  - *I'm confused and don't know what to do.*
  - *I'm afraid to get close to people.*
  - *This isn't the real world.*
  - *I'm afraid I might never stop crying.*
  - *I'm afraid I'll lose control.*

- **Working With Intense Emotions In All Members At Once**
  - Once this has occurred, you must make a decision as to which member to work with.
    - *Bring the focus back to one person.*
    - *Move next to the person who is crying.*
    - *You can pair people up to work together.*

- **Working With Projections and Other Problems of Self-Awareness**
  - *I can't talk to my parents.*
  - *My father wouldn't talk in English.*
  - *Here let me help you.*
  - *A great part of me wants this, and a part of me wants that.*
  - *I so much want your approval.*
  - *I feel very empty.*
  - *I feel unappreciated.*
  - *I don't like being overweight.*
  - *What I get out of that is_____.*

SECTION IV: The Final Stage

- **Tasks to Accomplish**
  - Members are encouraged to face the inevitable ending of the group and to discuss fully their feelings of separation.
  - Members are encouraged to complete any unfinished business they have with their members or the leaders

- Members are taught how to leave the group and how to carry with them what they have learned and especially how to talk to significant people in their lives.
- Leaders help members discover ways of creating their own support systems after they leave the group.
- Specific plans for follow up work and evaluation are made.
- Consideration is given to how members might discount a group experience and to teach members relapse prevention techniques.

- **Summing Up**
- **Dealing with Unfinished Work**
- **Arranging Homework Assignments**
- **Leaders Comments to Members**
- **Terminating the Group**
  - **Preparing for Termination**
    - Reviewing the highlights of the group experience.
    - Expressing unacknowledged aspects of group experience.
    - Exploring the issue of separation.
    - Rehearsing new roles.
    - Being specific about outcomes and plans.
    - Projecting the future.
    - Summarizing personal reactions to the group.
    - Making contracts

- **Continued Assessment and Follow Up**
  - Encouraging Contact with Other Group Members
  - Arranging a Follow up Session
  - Suggesting Further Work
- **Evaluating the Group**
  - Member Evaluation Form
  - Leader Evaluation Form

GUIDELINES AND SUGGESTIONS
FOR GROUP MEMBERS

- *Have a focus.* When you have focus, you find yourself committing to getting something productive from the group by focusing on what it is that you hope to accomplish. This includes clarifying any goals you may have, reviewing issues that you want explored or addressed, and specific changes you want to make. You will also clarify actions you would take to make these changes and can document it if it helps.

- *Be flexible.* Although it helps to approach the group with some idea of what you want to explore, don't be so committed to your agenda that you cannot deal spontaneously within the group. Be open to pursuing alternative paths if you are affected by others in your group.

- *Don't wait to work.* It is easy to let a group session go by without getting around to what you hope to do or say. The longer you wait to involve yourself, the harder it will become. Challenge yourself to say something at the beginning of each group, even if it's a brief statement of what it was like for you to come to the group that day.

- *Be "greedy."* The success of a group depends on your being eager to do your own work. This doesn't mean that you should monopolize time or be insensitive to the difficulty others may have in getting into the spotlight. But if you constantly wait until it's your turn, or try to monitor how much of the group's time should be allotted to you, you will inhibit the spontaneity and enthusiasm that can make a group exciting and productive.

- *Pay attention to feelings.* Intellectual discussions are great, but an experiential group is also about your feelings and convictions, not just you're thinking. Explore your life at an emotional level.

If you start sentences with, "I think…. Or "My opinion is…., you probably aren't exploring your life on a feeling level. Be open to letting yourself experience them as soon as you are in a session. Connect group discussions to yourself personally.

- *Express yourself.* Most of us are in the habit of censoring our expression of thoughts and feelings. We are afraid of being inappropriate or afraid that we will magnify our feelings. These fears are not unfounded but we do worse to ourselves if we do not verbalize them. A group is an ideal place to find out what would happen if we said what was in our minds. If you have feelings that relate to the group, be willing to express them.

- *Be an active participant.* You will help yourself most if you participate in the group. Members who are silent observers benefit less than members who participate.

- *Experiment.* Look at the group as a place in which you are safer and freer to express yourself in different ways and try out different sides to you. Then you can carry these new behaviors into the outside world. Then you can report to the group how you are behaving differently outside.

- *Be willing explore.* No matter how well your life is going now, it can be enriched by the opportunity to explore your feelings, values, beliefs, attitudes, and thoughts and to consider changes you may want to make. Even if you do not have a pressing issue in your life, assume that the issues that come up for you are worth exploring.

- *Don't expect change to be instantaneous.* If you do seek change in your life, remember that such changes do not usually happen all at once or without some backsliding. Don't be overly critical of yourself if you experience setbacks. Realize that it will take time to change longstanding patterns and there might be a tendency to revert to familiar ways when you are faced with stressful, situations. Give yourself credit that you are willing to try and aim for small changes that you can see yourself making.

- ***Don't expect others to appreciate your changes.*** Some people in your life may have an investment in keeping you the way you are now. You may find less support for your struggles outside the group than in it. Use the group to explore ways to handle any resistance you may encounter outside. It is a good idea to remind yourself that you are in this group primarily to make all the changes you want to make in yourself, not to change someone else.

- ***Don't expect to be fully understood within the group.*** Groups heighten a sense of intimacy and provide opportunity for being understood by others; however, it is unlikely that you will be fully understood. Members will see certain dimensions of you but will not have a good idea of what you are like otherwise. You don't have to qualify and footnote everything you say. If you decide to explore a relationship you are in, better not to focus on giving a full detailed picture of it, you will be talking forever. Better to resign yourself in advance to the idea that others won't and can't have the full picture.

- ***Don't expect to fully understand others in the group.*** You do a disservice to others in the group if you suppose that you have them all figured out. Like you, they are presumably working on expressing a side of themselves that they do not have an opportunity to express. People are very complex.

- ***Stick with one feeling at a time.*** Try to immediately express your feeling when you feel it. Try not to censor one feeling because you are feeling a contradictory one. You may have mixed emotions about an issue, but I you fully want to face that issue, try to stick with those feelings one at a time.

- *Avoid advising, interpreting and questioning.* As you listen to others in that group, you will often be tempted to offer advice. Too much advice can inundate people. You are in the group to express yourself. The people could begin to withdraw if they get too much advice. Express your feelings and experiences of your own that the person stimulated. Similarly, sometimes everyone takes on the role of the group leader in interpreting the speaker. Here the speaker can get defensive feeling like she is the only one working on an issue. People also get defensive when faced with an onslaught of questions. Questions can be asked that open people up rather than shut them down. If you want to ask a question, preface it by saying why you are interested. Let others know of your personal interest in hearing the answer. You can explore more if you tell them your personal reactions to the issue rather than questioning them about theirs.

- *Don't gossip.* Gossiping is talking about someone in the third person. If the person is not in the room, your group leader may encourage you to pretend that the person you want to talk about is in the room and have you speak directly to this person. This usually leads to a powerful expression of feelings and or thoughts. Try this… "I'm angry with him because…." Then say… "I'm angry with you because…." Which do you think will elicit more emotion?

- *Don't be quick to comfort.* If you rush too quickly to soothe someone's pain, you may be curtailing their ability and desire to fully express what they want to say. People grow from living through their pain so let them do it.

- *Give feedback.* When people express something that touches you, let them know by sharing your own feelings and reactions. Even if your feedback is not easy to express and may be difficult to listen to, it can be useful if it is delivered in a caring and respectful manner. It will engender trust in the group and leads you to honesty in your daily life. Rather than telling group members how to solve their problems, tell them about your own struggle with your own problems. Emphasize feedback that will give others a dearer sense of how their behavior affects you personally. Avoid judging people, but do let them know what specific behaviors of theirs might be getting in your way in dealing with them. Also let them know which behaviors might bring them closer to you.

- **Be open to feedback.** When others give you feedback about their reactions to your work, remember that, like you, they are there to try out new ways of expressing themselves directly. The most constructive approach is to listen and to think their reactions over until you get a grasp on what parts of it fit.

- **Avoid storytelling.** If you go on at length in providing information about you, you wind up distracting everyone, including yourself. Avoid narratives of your history. Express what is present, or express what you is past if are struggling with these events.

- **Exaggerate.** You can sometimes worry too much about whether you are genuine if you focus on a feeling that you have. Rather than wonder if you are exaggerating an emotion, give yourself permission to nurture them a bit and discover where they lead. Of course, you won't want to fake it, but you may get in touch with something genuine by throwing yourself into what you feel.

- **Avoid sarcasm.** A main goal of PARENTS is an experiential group is to learn to express feelings, including anger, in a direct manner. If you must be angry, say so directly. Do not use pot shots and sarcasm, which people don't know how to interpret. If you are hostile, which is indirect anger, not only does this negatively affect others around you but it also builds up inside you. If you learn to express even minor irritations there is a reduced risk that you will store up negative reactions that are unexpressed, which eventually lead to hostility and are expressed through sarcasm.

- *Include group leaders in your reactions.* It is normal for members to react to group leaders with feelings borrowed from the past, from fantasy, and from reality. You can turn this reaction to advantage by making it a special point to explore and express your feelings about your group leaders. Let them know how what they are saying and doing affects you.

- *Beware of labels.* Watch out for generalizations, summary statements and labels you use to describe yourself. Such self-imposed labels invite others to treat you as an outsider and insist on pigeonholing you for the duration of the group. Be ready to challenge others if you think they are reducing you to one dimension. Don't assume that labels tell you all there is to know about you or someone else.

- *Make friends with your defenses.* Your defenses have helped you get where you are today. They may need modification; come to understand your defenses by understanding how they protect you. You may sabotage your own work by saying things like I'm not smart. When you become aware of your typical patterns of avoidance, challenge these defenses and try to substitute direct and effective behavior.

- *Decide for yourself how much to disclose.* To find out about yourself, you need to take some risks by saying more than you are comfortable saying. Pushing yourself should be distinguished from disclosing things about yourself that you are doing simply because you think others expect it. Group is a good place to respect your own boundaries but it is also a place to respect them.

- ***Carry your work outside the group.*** You will find new ways of expressing yourself within the group. Try these behaviors out in everyday life with due respect for timing and with caution. Don't burden yourself with the expectation that you should disclose everything that you've disclosed to the group to a person in your life outside the group. You may role-play your father in the group. This does not mean that you have to role-play it with your actual father outside the group. Decide what you want to say to people outside the group. If you feel you want a closer relationship with your father, set behavioral goals for yourself outside the group that will help you get what you want.

- ***Don't be stopped by setbacks.*** You may have a specific vision of how you want to behave differently. But remember you may have relapses at times. Instead of getting discouraged and feeling that you will never change, be patient with temporary setbacks. Realize that you have spent years developing these patterns and when you are under pressure you may revert back to them even though they are old patterns and may not serve you well any longer.

- ***Express your feelings.*** Some feelings are easier to express than others. Groups usually focus on feelings that are causing members some difficulty. Try to talk about feelings that you frequently try to deny. Share not only feelings but share joys as well!

- ***Think about your thinking.*** Learn to monitor your self-talk. Identify those beliefs that that work against you. If you tell yourself that people don't like you, reflect on how easily you could be setting yourself up for defeat. You could be creating a host of self-fulfilling prophesies that keep you from feeling and acting the way you" like. Once you've identified these negative patterns, bring them to a session and begin to challenge them.

Learn to argue with those voices in your head that keep you from becoming the person you want to be.

- *Take responsibility for what you accomplish.* The leaders and members in your group will no doubt be interested in drawing you out. But remember that what you accomplish in the group is completely up to you. Don't wait for others to call on you. Learn to ask what you want. You will determine what and how much you get.

- *Be familiar with your culture.* Recognize that your cultural background will influence how you think and behave. Explore ways that you continue to be influenced by your background. Although there are some values that you appreciate that you have gotten from your culture, be open to questioning some of them. How would you like to modify some of them?

- *Develop a reading program.* Reading can be therapeutic and can also provide you with material that you can bring to group. Select books that will help you put your life experiences in perspective. Read books that teaches you knew patterns of thinking and behaving.

- *Write in your journal.* Writing in a journal will help you remember the experiences that you've had in group. If you rely on memory, chances are pretty good that you will forget. Even brief entries are helpful to monitor yourself and keep track of how well you are attaining your goals.

- *Respect confidentiality.* Keep in mind how easy it might be to betray the confidences of others. Make it a practice not to talk about group outside the group. If you talk about the group outside the group, talk about your own experiences. And what you are learning.

MODULE 3

Developmental Psychology

CHILD DEVELOPMENT

The Concept of Development

When a child meets certain developmental milestones of interest to researchers and parental figures, these will often be referred to as stages. Stages are considered a period of time which is often chronological by an individual's age, and refer to specific behaviors or physical characteristics that is qualitatively different from what it is at other ages. These differences can also be important in the sequence of developmental events which means that there are stages before and after the given stage which is identified by its own set of behavior and physical qualities.

Mechanisms of Development

Chronologically, developmental change runs parallel with age, however, age is not responsible solely for development. Genetic factors and environmental factors are the basic mechanisms associated with developmental change. Genetic factors can include concepts like cellular changes, which ultimately are responsible for overall growth in an individual, as well as vision and dietary needs amongst other genetic factors. Environmental factors can include concepts such as diet and disease exposure, as well as social, emotional and cognitive experiences.

Genetic and environmental factors often interact to cause developmental change in an individual. Some aspects of child development are notable for their plasticity, or the extent to which the direction of development is guided by environmental factors as well as initiated by genetic factors. When an aspect of development is strongly affected by early experience, it is said to show a high degree of plasticity; when the genetic make-up is the primary cause of development, plasticity is said to be low. Plasticity may involve guidance by endogenous factors like hormones as well as by exogenous factors like infection. What develops? What relevant aspects of the individual change over a period of time?

What are the rate and speed of development?

Milestones can be defined as the changes in specific physical and mental abilities. These can be changes such as walking and grasping different languages, and can conclude one developmental stage and the beginning of another. Milestones can be linked to indicate stage transitions. By studying developmental tasks, researchers have been able to understand what chronological age should be linked to which developmental milestones. However, there is a likelihood that there may be a variation in what has been completed in each milestone, even between children with developmental trajectories within the normal range.

In child development, a common concern in child development is developmental delays, which involve a delay in an age specific ability for important milestones. Developmental delays should be diagnosed by comparison with characteristic variability of a milestone, not with respect to average age at achievement. An example of a milestone would be eye-hand coordination, which includes a child's increasing ability to manipulate objects in a coordinated manner. Increased knowledge of age-specific milestones allows parents and others to keep track of appropriate development. Some noteworthy characteristics include physical growth and weight in a child to adult. When an individual continues to grow, so does the individuals proportions of the child's body (i.e large head and small toso and limbs to the adults small head and long torso and limbs.) The notion that is emphasized throughout this module is that while genetic factors play a major role in determining the growth rate, and particularly the changes in proportion characteristic of early human development, genetic factors can produce the maximum growth only if environmental conditions are adequate. Poor nutrition and frequent injury and disease can reduce the individual's adult stature, but the best environment cannot cause growth to a greater stature than is determined by heredity. Thus, it is important to remember that individual differences in developmental situations such as in height and weight during childhood are considerable. Some of these differences are due to family genetic factors, others to environmental factors.

Aspects of Child Development

Child development is not a matter of a single topic, but progresses somewhat differently for different aspects of the individual. Here are descriptions of the development of a number of physical and mental characteristics.

1. **Physical Growth and Individual Differences (Nature vs. Nurture)**

Physical growth in stature and weight occurs over the 15–20 years following birth, as the individual changes from the average weight of 3.5 kg and length of 50 cm at full term birth to full adult size. As stature and weight increase, the individual's proportions also change, from the relatively large head and small torso and limbs of the neonate, to the adult's relatively small head and long torso and limbs. The notion that is emphasized throughout this module is that while genetic factors play a major role in determining the growth rate, and particularly the changes in proportion characteristic of early human development, genetic factors can produce the maximum growth only if environmental conditions are adequate. Poor nutrition and frequent injury and disease can reduce the individual's adult stature, but the best environment cannot cause growth to a greater stature than is determined by heredity. Thus, it is important to remember that individual differences in developmental situations such as in height and weight during childhood are considerable. Some of these differences are due to family genetic factors, others to environmental factors.

2. **Motor Development**

Even when a child learns to walk also varies. Abilities for physical movement change through childhood from the largely reflexive (unlearned, involuntary) movement patterns of the young infant to the highly skilled voluntary movement's characteristic of later childhood and adolescence. These also vary within children and are based on biological as well as environmental factors. Normal individual differences in motor ability are common and depend in part on the child's weight and build. However, after the infant period, normal individual differences are strongly affected by opportunities to practice, observe, and be instructed on specific movements.

3. **Language**

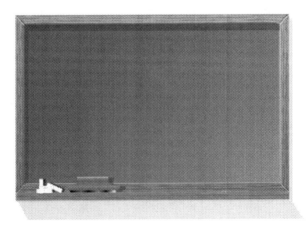

Although the role of adult discourse is important in facilitating the child's learning, there is considerable disagreement amongst theorists about the extent to which children's early meanings and expressive words arises directly from adult input as opposed to intrinsic factors relating to the child's cognitive functions. Findings about the initial mapping of new words, the ability to decontextualize words and refine meaning are diverse. In one model, although parental input has a critical role, children rely on cognitive processing to establish subsequent use of words. However, naturalistic research on language development has indicated that preschoolers' vocabularies are strongly associated with the number of words addressed to them by adults.

There is as yet no single accepted theory of language acquisition. Current explanations vary in emphasis from learning theory, with its emphasis on reinforcement and imitation (Skinner), to biological, nativist theories, with innate underlying mechanisms (Chomsky and Pinker), to a more interactive approach within a social context (Piaget and Tomasello).

4. **Cultural Differences**

Regardless of the culture a baby is born into, they are born with a few core domains of knowledge. These principals allow him or her to make sense of their environment and learn upon previous experience by using motor skills such as grasping or crawling. There are some population differences in motor development, with girls showing some advantages in small muscle usage, including articulation of sounds with lips and tongue. Ethnic differences in reflex movements of newborn infants have been reported, suggesting that some biological factor is at work. Cultural differences may encourage learning of motor skills like using the left hand only for sanitary purposes and the right hand for all other uses, producing a population difference. Cultural factors are also seen at work in practiced voluntary movements such as the use of the foot to dribble a soccer ball or the hand to dribble a basketball.

5. **Cognitive -Intellectual Development**

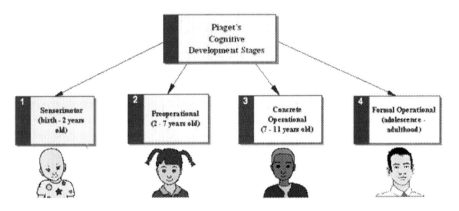

The capacity to learn, remember, and symbolize information, and to solve problems, exists at a simple level in young infants, who can perform cognitive tasks such as discriminating animate and inanimate beings or recognizing small numbers of objects. During childhood, learning and information-processing increase in speed, memory becomes increasingly longer, and symbol use and the capacity for abstraction develop until a near-adult level is reached by adolescence. Cognitive development has genetic and other biological mechanisms, as is seen in the many genetic causes of mental retardation. Environmental factors including food and nutrition, responsiveness of parents, daily experiences, physical activity and love can also influence early brain development of children.

6. Social-Emotional Development

Newborn infants do not seem to experience fear or have preferences for contact with any specific people. In the first few months they only experience happiness, sadness, and anger... A baby's first smile usually occurs between 6 and 10 weeks. It is called a 'social smile' because it usually occurs during social interactions. By about 8–12 months, they go through a fairly rapid change and become fearful of perceived threats; they also begin to prefer familiar people and show anxiety and distress when separated from them or approached by strangers. Separation anxiety is a normal stage of development to an extent. Kicking, screaming, and throwing temper tantrums are perfectly normal symptoms for separation anxiety. Depending on the level of intensity, one may determine whether or not a child has separation anxiety disorder. This is when a child constantly refuses to separate from the parent, but in an intense manner. This can be given special treatment but the parent usually cannot do anything about the situation.

The capacity for empathy and the understanding of social rules begin in the preschool period and continue to develop into adulthood. Middle childhood is characterized by friendships with age-mates, and adolescence by emotions connected with sexuality and the beginnings of romantic love. Anger seems most intense during the toddler and early preschool period and during adolescence.

Thus, while genetic factors appear to regulate some social-emotional developments that occur at predictable ages, such as fearfulness, and attachment to familiar people. Experience plays a role in determining which people are familiar, which social rules are obeyed, and how anger is expressed.

7. Emotional Intelligence

Parenting practices have been shown to predict children's emotional intelligence. The objective is to study the time mothers and children spent together in joint activity, the types of activities that they develop when they are together, and the relation that those activities have with the children's trait emotional intelligence. The amount of time mothers spent with their children and the quality of their interactions are important in terms of children's trait emotional intelligence, not only because those times of joint activity reflect a more positive parenting, but because they are likely to promote modeling, reinforcement, shared attention, and social cooperation.

8. Socioeconomic Status

Socioeconomic status is measured primarily based on the factors of income, educational attainment and occupation. Current investigations into the role of socioeconomic factors on child development repeatedly show that continual poverty is more harmful on IQ, and cognitive abilities than short-lived poverty. Children in families who experience persistent financial hardships and poverty have significantly impaired cognitive abilities compared to those in families who do not face this issue. Low income poverty can cause a number of further issues shown to effect child development, such as malnutrition and lead poisoning due to lead paint found on the walls of some houses.

Parental educational attainment is the most significant socioeconomic factor in predicting the child's cognitive abilities; those with a mother with high IQ are likely to have a child with a higher IQ. Similarly, maternal occupation is associated with better cognitive achievement.

Risk Factors for Poor Child Development

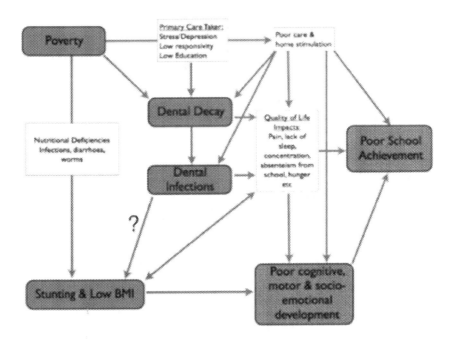

Child development can be negatively influenced by a number of environmental risk factors, many of which have been studied in developing countries. Malnutrition and lack of certain nutrients in a child's diet, postpartum depression, maternal depression in general and maternal substance abuse are but a few of these factors, which have received particular attention by researchers; however, many more factors have been considered.

In sum, stages of development may overlap or be associated with specific other aspects of development, such as speech or movement. However, even within a particular developmental area, transition into a stage may not mean that the previous stage is completely finished. For example, in Erikson's discussion of stages of personality, this theorist suggests that a lifetime is spent in reworking issues that were originally characteristic of a childhood stage. Similarly, the theorist of cognitive development, Piaget, described situations in which children could solve one type of problem using mature thinking skills, but could not accomplish this for less familiar problems, a phenomenon he called horizontal decal age.

NOTES:

THE CLASSICAL THEORISTS

There are major classical theorists who have discussed child development. The reason is that it is important to understand that children do not develop at the same pace. Children think differently than adults. Sometimes parents believe that if they use their adult reasoning, that their children will understand. However children often simply do not have the biological, cognitive or social abilities yet.

The theorists discussed in the following sections are:

Freud and Psychosexual Development
Erikson and Psychosocial Development
Piaget and Cognitive Development
Kohlberg and Moral Development
Bowlby and Attachment Theory.

FREUD

PSYCHOSEXUAL STAGES

Freud discussed five psychosexual stages of development: Oral, Anal, Phallic, Latency and Genital. The child, in pursuing and satisfying his or her libido (sexual drive), could experience failure through parental and societal disapproval. As a result the child could associate anxiety with the given erogenous zone. To avoid anxiety, the child becomes fixated or preoccupied with the psychological themes related to that particular erogenous zone. These anxieties might persist into adulthood, and underlie the personality and psychopathology of the man or woman, as neurosis, hysteria, personality disorders, etc. So that during each stage, if the parents did not provide satisfying interactions with the child, the child could experience anxiety in that zone. This anxiety surrounding the specific zone would follow the child into adulthood where the child would experience certain personality traits.

Stage	Age Range	Erogenous Zone	Consequences of Psychological Fixation
Oral	Birth–1 year	Mouth	Orally aggressive: chewing gum and the ends of pencils, etc. Orally Passive: smoking, eating, kissing, oral sexual practices Oral stage fixation might result in a passive, Gullible, immature, manipulative personality.
Anal	1–3 years	Bowel and bladder elimination	Anal retentive: Obsessively organized, or excessively neat anal expulsive: reckless, careless, defiant, disorganized, coprophilous
Phallic	3–6 years	Genitals	Oedipus complex (in boys and girls); According to Sigmund Freud. Electra complex (in girls); according to Carl Jung.

		Dormant sexual feelings	Sexual fulfillment if fixation occurs in this stage.
Latency	6–puberty	Dormant sexual feelings	Sexual fulfillment if fixation occurs in this stage.
Genital	Puberty–death	Sexual interests mature	Frigidity, impotence, unsatisfactory relationships

A. The Oral Stage of Psychosexual Development

The first stage of psychosexual development is the oral stage, spanning from birth until the age of two years. In this stage, the infant's mouth is the focus of gratification derived from the pleasure of feeding at the mother's breast, and also from the oral exploration of his or her environment, i.e. the tendency to place objects in the mouth.

In this stage, governed by the Pleasure Principle (I want or I don't want), the id dominates. Because neither the ego nor the super ego is yet fully developed, and, since the infant has no personality (identity), every action is based upon the pleasure principle. Nonetheless, the infantile ego is forming during the oral stage.

Two factors contribute to the formation of the infantile ego:

1. in developing a body image, she is discrete from the external world, e.g. the child understands pain when it is applied to his or her body, thus identifying the physical boundaries between body and environment;
2. Experiencing delayed gratification leads to understanding that specific behaviors satisfy some needs, e.g. crying gratifies certain needs.

The key experience in the infant's oral stage of psychosexual development is weaning. This represents the child's first feeling of loss because she is losing the physical intimacy of feeding at mother's breast. Also, weaning increases the infant's self-awareness in that she does not control the environment. Here the infant learns of delayed gratification. This in turn leads to the formation of the capacities for **independence** (awareness of the limits of the self) and **trust** (behaviors leading to gratification). Yet, if there is a problem in the oral-stage — too much or too little gratification of desire — then this might lead to an oral-stage fixation, characterized by passivity, gullibility, immaturity, unrealistic optimism. According to Freud, this is manifested in a manipulative personality consequent to ego malformation. In the case of too much gratification, the child does not learn that he or she does not control the environment, and that gratification is not always immediate, thereby forming an immature personality. In the case of too little gratification, the infant might become passive upon learning that gratification is not forthcoming, despite having produced the gratifying behavior.

B. The Anal Stage of Psychosexual Development

The second stage of psychosexual development is the anal stage. This spans the age of eighteen months to three years. In this stage, the infant's erogenous zone changes from the mouth to the anus and the ego formation continues. Toilet training is the child's key anal-stage experience, occurring at about the age of two years. This can result in conflict between the Id (demanding immediate gratification) and the Ego (demanding delayed gratification) in eliminating bodily wastes. Ego is governed by the Reality Principle and says I can or I can't. The style of parenting influences the resolution of the Id–Ego conflict, which can be either gradual or psychologically uneventful, or which can be sudden and psychologically traumatic. The ideal resolution of the Id–Ego conflict is in the child's adjusting to some parental demands that teach the value and importance of physical cleanliness and environmental order, ultimately producing a self-controlled adult. Yet, if the parents make big demands of the child, by over-emphasizing toilet training, it might lead to the development of a compulsive personality, a person too concerned with neatness and order. If the child obeys the Id, and the parents yield, he or she might develop a self-indulgent personality characterized by personal laziness and environmental disorder. If the parents respond to that, the child must comply, but might develop a weak sense of self, because it was the parents' will, and not the child's ego, who controlled the toilet training.

C. The Phallic Stage of Psychosexual Development

The third stage of psychosexual development is the phallic stage this occurs between the ages of three to six years. During this stage, the child's genitalia are his or her primary erogenous zone. It is in this third developmental stage that children become aware of their bodies, the bodies of other children, and the bodies of their parents. At times, they may gratify physical curiosity by undressing and exploring each other and their genitals, and so learn the biological (sexual) differences between the genders and the gender differences between "boy" and "girl". In the phallic stage, boys undergo what Freud calls the psychosexual experience of the Oedipus complex. Here there is a competition for attentions and possession of mother. This psychological complex derives from the 5th-century BC Greek character, Oedipus, who unwittingly killed his father and sexually possessed his mother. Similarly, in the phallic stage, a girl's decisive psychosexual experience is the Electra complex. Here there is an unconscious desire for psychosexual possession of father. This psychological complex derives from the 5th-century BC Greek mythological Electra, who plotted matricidal revenge with her brother, against their mother, and their stepfather, for their murder of Agamemnon, their father.

It was Freud's student and collaborator, Carl Jung, who actually coined the term **Electra complex** in 1913. Freud rejected Jung's term as psychoanalytically inaccurate: "that what we have said about the Oedipus complex applies with complete strictness to the male child only, and that we are right in rejecting the term 'Electra complex', which seeks to emphasize the analogy between the attitudes of the two sexes".

At some point, the boy realizes that he cannot possess his mother because the father doe and the boy because of castration anxiety, gives up on this notion.

Whereas boys develop castration anxiety, girls develop penis envy, believing that without a penis, she cannot sexually possess mother, as the infantile id demands. Resultantly, the girl redirects her desire for sexual union upon father. She then moves toward heterosexual femininity that culminates in bearing a child who replaces the absent penis. Moreover, after the phallic stage, the girl's psychosexual development includes transferring her primary erogenous zone from the infantile clitoris to the adult vagina.

Therefore, the satisfactory parental handling and through the resolution of the Oedipus and Electra Complex, the infantile super-ego develops, because, by identifying with a parent, the child internalizes morality, thereby, choosing to comply with societal rules, rather than having to reflexively comply in fear of punishment.

D. The Latency Stage of Psychosexual Development

The fourth stage of psychosexual development is the latency stage that spans from the age of six years until puberty. In this stage, the child consolidates the character habits he or she developed in the three, earlier stages of psychological and sexual development. Here the child derives the pleasure of gratification from secondary process-thinking that directs the libidinal drives toward external activities, such as schooling, friendships, hobbies, etc.

E. The Genital Stage of Psychosexual Development

The fifth stage of psychosexual development is the genital stage. This stage spans puberty and adult life, and thus occupies most of the life of a man and of a woman. The purpose of this stage is the psychological detachment and independence from the parents. The genital stage affords the person the ability to confront and resolve his or her remaining psychosexual childhood conflicts. As in the phallic stage, the genital stage is centered upon the genitalia, but here the sexuality is social and adult, rather than solitary and infantile. In this stage, the person's concern shifts from primary-drive gratification (instinct) to applying secondary process-thinking to gratify desire symbolically and intellectually by means of friendships, a love relationship, family and adult responsibilities.

ERIKSON
PSYCHOSOCIAL STAGES OF DEVELOPMENT

Erikson was a Neo-Freudian. He extended Freud's stages from birth until death. He believed that development occurred throughout the life span. He has been described as an "ego psychologist" studying the stages of development, spanning the entire lifespan. Each of Erikson's stages of psychosocial development is marked by a conflict for which successful resolution will result in a favorable outcome, and by an important event that this conflict resolves itself around. Favorable resolution of each stage are sometimes known as "virtues." Erikson's suggested that each individual must learn how to hold both extremes of each specific life-stage challenge in tension with one another, not rejecting one end of the tension or the other. Only when both extremes in a life-stage challenge are understood and accepted as both required and useful, can the optimal virtue for that stage surface. Thus, 'trust' and 'miss-trust' must both be understood and accepted, in order for realistic 'hope' to emerge as a viable solution at the first stage. Similarly, 'integrity' and 'despair' must both be understood and embraced, in order for actionable 'wisdom' to emerge as a viable solution at the last stage.

The Erikson life-stage virtues, in order of the eight stages in which they may be acquired, are:

A. **Basic Trust vs. Basic Mistrust. Infancy to 1 year of age.**

Whether or not the baby develops basic trust or basic mistrust is not merely a matter of nurture. It depends on the quality of the maternal relationship. The mother carries out and reflects their inner perceptions of trustworthiness, a sense of personal meaning, etc. on the child. If successful in this, the baby develops a sense of trust, which "forms the basis in the child for a sense of identity".

B. **Autonomy vs. Shame. Early childhood.**

Introduces the concept of autonomy vs. shame and doubt. During this stage the child is trying to master toilet training.

C. **Purpose - Initiative vs. Guilt. Preschool to 3–6 years**.

Does the child have the ability to or do things on their own, such as dress him or herself? If "guilty" about making his or her own choices, the child will not function well. Erikson has a positive outlook on this stage, saying that most guilt is quickly compensated by a sense of accomplishment.

D. **Competence- Industry vs. Inferiority. School-age to 6-11.**

Here the child compares his or her self-worth to others (such as in a classroom environment). The child can recognize major disparities in personal abilities relative to other children. Erikson places some emphasis on the teacher, who should ensure that children do not feel inferior.

E. Identity vs. Role Confusion. Adolescent 12 years till 20.

The youngster questions his or her sense of self. Who am I, how do I fit in? Where am I going in life? Erikson believes, that if the parents allow the child to explore, she will conclude his or her own identity. However, if the parents continually push him/her to conform to their views, the teen will face identity confusion.

F. Intimacy vs. Isolation. Ages 20 to 24.

This is the first stage of adult development. This development usually happens during young adulthood, which is between the ages of Dating, marriage, family and friendships are important during the stage in their life. By successfully forming loving relationships with other people, individuals are able to experience love and intimacy. Those who fail to form lasting relationships may feel isolated and alone.

G. Generativity vs. Stagnation. Ages 25-64.

This is the second stage of adulthood. During this time people are normally settled in their life and know what is important to them. In this stage, a person either makes progress in their career or treads lightly in their career and feels unsure if this is what they want to do for the rest of their working lives. Also during this time, a person is enjoying raising their children and participating in activities. This gives them a sense of purpose. If a person is not comfortable with the way their life is progressing, they may be regretful about the decisions and feel a sense of uselessness.

H. **Ego integrity vs. Despair. Ages 65 and on.**

During this time an individual has reached the last chapter in their life and retirement is approaching or has already taken place. Many people, who have achieved what was important to them, look back on their lives and feel great accomplishment and a sense of integrity. Conversely, those who had a difficult time during middle adulthood may look back and feel a sense of despair.

On ego identity versus role confusion, ego identity enables each person to have a sense of individuality, or as Erikson would say, "Ego identity, then, in its subjective aspect, is the awareness of the fact that there is a self-sameness and continuity to the ego's synthesizing methods and a continuity of one's meaning for others" (1963). Role confusion, however, is, according to Barbara Engler in her book *Personality Theories* (2006), "the inability to conceive of oneself as a productive member of one's own society". This inability to conceive of oneself as a productive member is a great danger; it can occur during adolescence, when looking for an occupation.

PIAGET
COGNITIVE DEVELOPMENT

Piaget studied cognitive development in children. He proposed 4 stages of cognitive development. They are:

A. **Sensorimotor:** (birth to about age 2)

In this stage, the child learns about himself and his environment through motor and reflex actions. Thought derives from sensation and movement. The child learns that she is separate from his or her environment and that aspects of his/her environment—his parents or favorite toy—continue to exist even though they might be outside the reach of his senses. This is called object permanence. During this stage, learning for a child should be geared to the sensorimotor system. For example, a parent can modify behavior by using the senses: a frown, a stern or soothing voice.

B. **Preoperational:** (begins about the time the child starts to talk to about age 7)

Now the child has language. Applying his new knowledge of language, the child begins to use symbols to represent objects. Early in this stage she personifies objects, meaning they are now better able to think about things and events that are not immediately present. During this stage, because of a present focus, children have difficulty conceptualizing time. Their thinking is influenced by fantasy—the way they'd like things to be. This stage is characterized by egocentrism. They assume that others see situations the same way they do. They take in information and change it in their mind to fit their ideas. Using neutral words, body outlines and equipment, a child can touch gives him an active role in learning? Here a child still cannot grasp the concept of conservation - an ability to understand that specific properties of objects such as volume, weight or number remains the same despite the changes in shape or arrangement of those objects.

C. **Concrete:** (about first grade to early adolescence)

During this stage, accommodation increases. The child develops an ability to think abstractly and to make rational judgments about concrete or observable phenomena. In the past she needed to manipulate physically to understand. In teaching this child, giving him the opportunity to ask questions and to explain things back to you, a parent allows him or her the chance to mentally manipulate information.

D. **Formal operations:**

According to Piaget, this stage brings cognitive development to its final form. This person no longer requires concrete objects to make rational judgments. At this point, she is capable of hypothetical and deductive reasoning. Interactions for the adolescent may be wide-ranging because she'll be able to consider many possibilities from several perspectives.

Piaget's Stages of Moral Development

Piaget studied many aspects of moral judgment, but most of his findings fit into a two-stage theory.

1. Children younger than 10 or 11 years think about moral dilemmas one way; while older children think about them differently. Younger children regard rules as fixed and absolute. They believe that rules are handed down by adults or by God and cannot be changed.
2. The older child's view is more relativistic. She understands that it is permissible to change rules if everyone agrees. Rules are not sacred and absolute. They are devices, which humans use to get along cooperatively.

At approximately the same time, 10 or 11 years, children's moral thinking undergoes other shifts. Younger children base their moral judgments more on consequences. Older children base their judgments on intentions. When, for example, the young child hears about one boy who broke 15 cups trying to help his mother and another boy who broke only one cup trying to steal cookies, the younger child thinks that the first boy did worse. The child primarily considers the amount of damage--the consequences--whereas the older child is more likely to judge wrongness in terms of the motives underlying the act (Piaget, 1932, p. 137).

Piaget essentially found a series of changes that occur between the ages of 10 and 12, just when the child begins to enter the general stage of formal operations.

Intellectual development, however, does not stop at this point. This is just the beginning of formal operations, which continue to develop at least until age 16. Accordingly, one might expect thinking about moral issues to continue to develop throughout adolescence.

KOHLBERG
MORAL DEVLOPMENT

Kohlberg focused on moral development and proposed a stage theory of moral thinking, which goes well beyond Piaget's initial formulations. He interviewed both children and adolescents about moral dilemmas, and he did find stages that go well beyond Piaget's. He uncovered six stages, only the first three of which share many features with Piaget's stages.

KOHLBERG'S SIX STAGES:

Level 1. Preconvention Morality

Stage 1. Obedience and Punishment Orientation.

Kohlberg's stage 1 is similar to Piaget's first stage of moral thought. The child assumes that powerful authorities hand down a fixed set of rules, which the child must obey.

Kohlberg presented the children with several dilemmas, the most famous of which is The Heinz Dilemma. Kohlberg was not interested in the child's decision of right or wrong; but rather why the child thought the decision was right or wrong.

To briefly summarize one of Kohlberg's dilemmas, *Heinz's wife was deathly ill. She needed medication to survive. Heinz went to the druggist to buy the medication. It was much too expensive. Heinz did not have the money and the druggist would not give him the medicine. Later that evening, Heinz broke into the pharmacy and stole the medicine.*

Was Heinz right or wrong? To the Heinz dilemma, the child at Stage 1 typically says that Heinz was wrong to steal the drug because "It's against the law," or "It's bad to steal." When asked to elaborate, the child usually responds in terms of the consequences involved, explaining that stealing is bad "because you'll get punished" (Kohlberg, 1958b).

Kohlberg calls stage 1 thinking "preconvention" because children do not yet speak as members of society. Instead, they see morality as something external to themselves, as that which the adults say they must do.

Stage 2. Individualism and Exchange.

During this stage children recognize that there is not just one right view that is handed down by the authorities. Different individuals have different viewpoints. "Heinz," they might point out, "might think its right to take the drug, the druggist would not." Since everything is *relative,* each person is free to pursue his or her *individual* interests.

Children at both stages 1 and 2 talk about punishment; however, they perceive it differently. At stage 1 punishment is tied up in the child's mind with wrongness; punishment "proves" that disobedience is wrong. At stage 2, in contrast, punishment is simply a risk that one naturally wants to avoid.

Stage 2 respondents have some sense of right action. This is a notion of *fair exchange* or fair deals. The philosophy is one of returning favors-- "If you scratch my back, I'll scratch yours." To the Heinz story, subjects often say that Heinz was right to steal the drug because the druggist was unwilling to make a fair deal; he was "trying to rip Heinz off,"

Children at stage 2 are still said to reason at the preconvention level because they speak as individuals rather than as members of society.

They see people exchanging favors, but there is still no identification with the values of the family or community.

Level II. Conventional Morality

Stage 3. Good Interpersonal Relationships.

At this stage children--who are by now usually entering their teens--see morality as more than simple deals. They believe that people should live up to the expectations of the family and community. Good behavior means having good motives and interpersonal feelings such as love, empathy, trust, and concern for others.

As mentioned earlier, there are similarities between Kohlberg's first three stages and Piaget's two stages. In both sequences there is a shift from unquestioning obedience to a relativistic outlook and to a concern for good motives. For Kohlberg, however, these shifts occur in three stages rather than two.

Stage 4. Maintaining the Social Order.

Stage 3 reasoning works best in two-person relationships with family members or close friends, where one can make a real effort to get to know feelings and needs of others and try to help. At stage 4, in contrast, the children become more broadly concerned with *society as a whole.* The emphasis now is on obeying laws, respecting authority, and performing one's duties so that the social order is maintained. Here children make moral decisions from the perspective of society as a whole.

Level III. Post-conventional Morality

Stage 5. Social Contract and Individual Rights. At stage 4, people want to keep society functioning. However, a smoothly functioning society is not necessarily a good one. A totalitarian society might be well organized, but it is hardly the moral ideal. At stage 5, people begin to ask, "What makes for a good society?" They begin to think about society in a very theoretical way, stepping back from their own society and considering the rights and values that a society ought to uphold. They then evaluate existing societies in terms of these prior considerations. They are said to take a "prior-to-society" perspective (Colby and Kohlberg, 1983, p. 22).

Stage 5 respondents basically believe that a good society is best conceived as a social contract into which people freely enter to work toward the benefit of all they recognize that different social groups within a society will have different values, but they believe that all rational people would agree on two points.

First they would all want certain basic *rights,* such as liberty and life, to be protected second, they would want some *democratic* procedures for changing unfair law and for improving society.

It is in this case that usually the moral and legal standpoints coincide and conflict. The judge should weight the moral standpoint more heavily but preserve the legal law in punishing Heinz lightly. (Kohlberg, 1976, p. 38)

Stage 5 subjects, then, talk about "morality" and "rights" that take some priority over particular laws. Kohlberg insists, however, that we do not judge people to be at stage 5 merely from their verbal labels. We need to look at their social perspective and mode of reasoning. At stage 4, too, subjects frequently talk about the "right to life," but for them this right is legitimized by the authority of their social or religious group (e.g., by the Bible). Presumably, if their group valued property over life, they would too. At stage 5, people make more of an independent effort to think out what any society ought to value. They often reason, for example, that property has little meaning without life. They are trying to determine logically what a society should to be like (Kohlberg, 1981, pp. 21-22; Gibbs et al., 1983, p. 83).

Stage 6: Universal Principles.

Stage 5 respondents are working toward a conception of the good society. They suggest that we need to (a) protect certain individual rights and (b) settle disputes through democratic processes. However, democratic processes alone do not always result in outcomes that we intuitively sense are just. A majority, for example, may vote for a law that hinders a minority. Thus, Kohlberg believes that there must be a higher stage; stage 6 that defines the principles by which we achieve justice.

Kohlberg's conception of justice follows that of the philosophers Kant and Rawls, as well as great moral leaders such as Gandhi and Martin Luther King. According to these theorists, the principles of justice require us to treat the claims of all parties in an impartial manner, respecting the basic dignity, of all people as individuals. The principles of justice are therefore universal; they apply to all. Thus, for example, we would not vote for a law that aids some people but hurts others. The principles of justice guide us toward decisions based on an equal respect for all. In actual practice, Kohlberg says, we can reach just decisions by looking at a situation through one another's eyes.

It is probably true that the one issue that distinguishes stage 5 from stage 6 is civil disobedience. Stage 5 would be more hesitant to endorse civil disobedience because of its commitment to the social contract and to changing laws through democratic agreements. Only when an individual right is clearly at stake does violating the law seem justified. At stage 6, in contrast, a commitment to justice makes the rationale for civil disobedience stronger and broader.

Summary of Kohlberg:

At stage 1 children think that what is right is that which authority says is right. Doing the right thing is obeying authority and avoiding punishment. At stage 2, children are no longer so impressed by any single authority. They see that there are different sides to any issue. Since everything is relative, one is free to pursue one's own interests, although it is often useful to make deals and exchange favors with others.

At stages 3 and 4, young people think as members of the conventional society with its values, norms, and expectations. At stage 3, they emphasize being a good person, which basically means having helpful motives toward people close to one. At stage 4, the concern shifts toward obeying laws to maintain society as a whole.

At stages 5 and 6 people are less concerned with maintaining society for its own sake, and more concerned with the principles and values that make for a good society. At stage 5 they emphasize basic rights and the democratic processes that give everyone a say, and at stage 6 they define the principles that are most just.

NOTES:

Dr. Joan D. Atwood

BOWLBY
ATTACHMENT THEORY

Attachment theory, originating in the work of John Bowlby and developed by Mary Ainsworth, is a psychological, evolutionary and ethological theory that provides a descriptive and explanatory framework for understanding interpersonal relationships between human beings.

Infant Attachment:

Basically, the theory holds that infants become attached to individuals who are sensitive and responsive in social interactions with them, and who remain as consistent caregivers for some months during the period from about six months to two years of age. This is known as sensitive responsiveness. When an infant begins to crawl and walk, they begin to use attachment figures (familiar people) as a secure base to explore from and return to. Caregivers' responses lead to the development of patterns of attachment; these, in turn, lead to internal working models that guide the individual's perceptions, emotions, thoughts and expectations in later relationships. Separation anxiety or grief following the loss of an attachment figure is considered to be a normal and adaptive response for an attached infant. It is believed that these behaviors may have evolved because they increase the probability of survival of the child.

Research by developmental psychologist Mary Ainsworth in the 1960s and 70s reinforced the basic concepts, introduced the concept of the "secure base" and developed a theory of a number of attachment patterns in infants: secure attachment, avoidant attachment and anxious attachment. A fourth pattern, disorganized attachment, was identified later.

Within attachment theory, *attachment* means an affectional bond or tie between an individual and an attachment figure (usually a caregiver). Such bonds may be reciprocal between two adults, but between a child and a caregiver these bonds are based on the child's need for safety, security and protection. These needs are crucially important in infancy and childhood. The theory proposes that children attach to caretakers instinctively, for the purpose of survival and, ultimately, and eventually for genetic replication. The biological goal is survival and the psychological goal is security. In child-to-adult relationships, the child's tie is called the "attachment" and the caregiver's reciprocal equivalent is referred to as the "care-giving bond".

Infants form attachments to any consistent caregiver who is sensitive and responsive in social interactions with them. The quality of the social engagement is more influential than the amount of time spent. The role can be taken by anyone who consistently behaves in a "mothering" or caregiving way over a period of time. In attachment theory, this means a set of behaviors that involves engaging in lively social interaction with the infant and responding readily to signals and approaches.

Some infants direct attachment behavior (proximity seeking) toward more than one attachment figure almost as soon as they start to show discrimination between caregivers; most come to do so during their second year. These figures are arranged hierarchically, with the principal attachment figure at the top. The set-goal of the attachment behavioral system is to maintain a bond with an accessible and available attachment figure. "Alarm" is the term used for activation of the attachment behavioral system caused by fear of danger. "Anxiety" is the anticipation or fear of being cut off from the attachment figure. If the figure is unavailable or unresponsive, separation distress occurs. In infants, physical separation can cause anxiety and anger, followed by sadness and despair. By age three or four, physical separation is no longer such a threat to the child's bond with the attachment figure.

Threats to security in older children and adults arise from prolonged absence, breakdowns in communication, emotional unavailability, or signs of rejection or abandonment.

Attachment Behaviors:

A securely attached baby is free to concentrate on her or his environment.

The attachment behavioral system serves to maintain or achieve closer proximity to the attachment figure. Pre-attachment behaviors occur in the first six months of life. During the first phase (the first eight weeks), infants smile, babble, and cry to attract the attention of potential caregivers. Although infants of this age learn to discriminate between caregivers, these behaviors are directed at anyone in the vicinity. During the second phase (two to six months), the infant increasingly discriminates between familiar and unfamiliar adults, becoming more responsive toward the caregiver; following and clinging are added to the range of behaviors. Clear-cut attachment develops in the third phase, between the ages of six months and two years. The infant's behavior toward the caregiver becomes organized on a goal-directed basis to achieve the conditions that make it feel secure.

By the end of the first year, the infant is able to display a range of attachment behaviors designed to maintain proximity. These manifest as protesting the caregiver's departure, greeting the caregiver's return, clinging when frightened, and following when able. With the development of locomotion, the infant begins to use the caregiver or caregivers as a safe base from which to explore. Infant exploration is greater when the caregiver is present because the infant's attachment system is relaxed and she is free to explore. If the caregiver is inaccessible or unresponsive, attachment behavior is more strongly exhibited. Anxiety, fear, illness, and fatigue will cause a child to increase attachment behaviors.

After the second year, as the child begins to see the caregiver as an independent person, a more complex and goal-corrected partnership is formed. Children begin to notice others' goals and feelings and plan their actions accordingly. For example, whereas babies cry because of pain, two-year-olds cry to summon their caregiver, and if that does not work, cry louder, shout, or follow.

Attachment Patterns:

Ainsworth's work expanded the theory's concepts and enabled empirical testing of its tenets. Using Bowlby's early formulation, she conducted observational research on infant-parent pairs (or dyads) during the child's first year, combining extensive home visits with the study of behaviors in particular situations. Ainsworth identified three attachment styles, or patterns, that a child may have with attachment figures: secure, anxious-avoidant (insecure) and anxious-

Ambivalent or resistant (insecure).

Ainsworth's work in the United States attracted many scholars into the field, inspiring research and challenging the dominance of behaviorism. Further research by Mary Main and colleagues at the University of California, Berkeley identified a fourth attachment pattern, called disorganized disoriented attachment. The name reflects these children's lack of a coherent coping strategy.

The type of attachment developed by infants depends on the quality of care they have received. Each of the attachment patterns is associated with certain characteristic patterns of behavior, as described in the following table:

Child and Caregiver Behavior Patterns
before the Age of 18 Months.

Attachment Pattern	Child	Caregiver
Secure	Uses caregiver as a secure base for exploration. Protests caregiver's departure and seeks proximity and is comforted on return, returning to exploration. May be comforted by the stranger but shows clear preference for the caregiver.	Responds appropriately, promptly and consistently to needs. Caregiver has successfully formed a secure parental attachment bond to the child.
Avoidant	Little affective sharing in play. Little or no distress on departure, little or no visible response to return, ignoring or turning away with no effort to maintain contact if picked up. Treats the stranger similarly to the caregiver. The child feels that there is no attachment; therefore, the child is rebellious and has a lower self-image and self-esteem.	Little or no response to distressed child. Discourages crying and encourages independence.

Attachment Pattern	Child	Caregiver
Ambivalent Resistant	Unable to use caregiver as a secure base, seeking proximity before separation occurs. Distressed on separation with ambivalence, anger, reluctance to warm to caregiver and return to play on return. Preoccupied with caregiver's availability, seeking contact but resisting angrily when it is achieved. Not easily calmed by stranger. In this relationship, the child always feels anxious because the caregiver's availability is never consistent.	Inconsistent between appropriate and neglectful responses. Generally will -only respond after increased attachment behavior from the infant.
Disorganized	Stereotypies on return such as freezing or rocking. Lack of coherent attachment strategy shown by contradictory, disoriented behaviors such as approaching but with the back turned.	Frightened or frightening behavior, intrusiveness, withdrawal, negativity, role confusion, affective communication errors and maltreatment. Very often associated with many forms of abuse towards the child.

The presence of an attachment is distinct from its quality. Infants form attachments if there is someone to interact with, even if mistreated. Individual differences in the relationships reflect the history of care, as infants begin to predict the behavior of caregivers through repeated interactions. The focus is the pattern rather than quantity of attachment behaviors. Insecure attachment patterns are non-optimal as they can compromise exploration, self-confidence and mastery of the environment. However, insecure patterns are also adaptive, as they are suitable responses to caregiver unresponsiveness. For example, in the avoidant pattern, minimizing expressions of attachment even in conditions of mild threat may forestall alienating caregivers who are already rejecting, thus leaving open the possibility of responsiveness should a more serious threat arise.

Around 65% of children in the general population may be classified as having a secure pattern of attachment, with the remaining 35% being divided among the insecure classifications. Recent research has sought to ascertain the extent to which a parent's attachment classification is predictive of their children's classification. Parents' perceptions of their own childhood attachments were found to predict their children's classifications 75% of the time. Over the short term, the stability of attachment classifications is high, but becomes less so over the long term. It appears that stability of classification is linked to stability in caregiving conditions. Social stressors or negative life events—such as illness, death, abuse or divorce—are associated with instability of attachment patterns from infancy to early adulthood, particularly from secure to insecure. Conversely, these difficulties sometimes reflect particular upheavals in people's lives, which may change. Sometimes, parents' responses change as the child develops, changing classification from insecure to secure. Fundamental changes can and do take place after the critical early period. Physically abused and neglected children are less likely to develop secure attachments, and their insecure classifications tend to persist through the pre-school years.

Neglect alone is associated with insecure attachment organizations, and rates of disorganized attachment are markedly elevated in maltreated infants.

This situation is complicated by difficulties in assessing attachment classification in older age groups. The Strange Situation procedure is for ages 12 to 18 months only; adapted versions exist for pre-school children. Techniques have been developed to allow verbal ascertainment of the child's state of mind with respect to attachment. An example is the "stem story", in which a child is given the beginning of a story that raises attachment issues and asked to complete it. For older children, adolescents and adults, semi-structured interviews are used in which the manner of relaying content may be as significant as the content itself. However, there are no substantially validated measures of attachment for middle childhood or early adolescence (approximately 7 to 13 years of age).

Some authors have questioned the idea that a taxonomy of categories representing a qualitative difference in attachment relationships can be developed. Examination of data from 1,139 15-month-olds showed that variation in attachment patterns was continuous rather than grouped. This criticism introduces important questions for attachment typologies and the mechanisms behind apparent types. However, it has relatively little relevance for attachment theory itself, which "neither requires nor predicts discrete patterns of attachment".

Possible Consequences of Early Attachment Patterns:

There is an extensive body of research demonstrating a significant association between attachment organizations and children's functioning across multiple domains. Early insecure attachment does not necessarily predict difficulties, but it is a liability for the child, particularly if similar parental behaviors continue throughout childhood. Compared to that of securely attached children, the adjustment of insecure children in many spheres of life is not as soundly based, putting their future relationships in jeopardy. Although the link is not fully established by research and there are other influences besides attachment, secure infants are more likely to become socially competent than their insecure peers. Relationships formed with peers influence the acquisition of social skills, intellectual development and the formation of social identity.

Classification of children's peer status (popular, neglected or rejected) has been found to predict subsequent adjustment. Insecure children, particularly avoidant children, are especially vulnerable to family risk. Their social and behavioral problems increase or decline with deterioration or improvement in parenting. However, an early secure attachment appears to have a lasting protective function. As with attachment to parental figures, subsequent experiences may alter the course of development.

The most concerning pattern is disorganized attachment. About 80% of maltreated infants are likely to be classified as disorganized, as opposed to about 12% found in non-maltreated samples. Only about 15% of maltreated infants are likely to be classified as secure. Children with a disorganized pattern in infancy tend to show markedly disturbed patterns of relationships. Subsequently their relationships with peers can often be characterized by a "fight or flight" pattern of alternate aggression and withdrawal. Affected maltreated children are also more likely to become maltreating parents. A minority of maltreated children do not, instead achieving secure attachments, good relationships with peers and non-abusive parenting styles. The link between insecure attachment, particularly the disorganized classification, and the emergence of childhood psychopathology is well-established, although it is a non-specific risk factor for future problems, not a pathology or a direct cause of pathology in itself. In the classroom, it appears that ambivalent children are at an elevated risk for internalizing disorders, and avoidant and disorganized children, for externalizing disorders.

One explanation for the effects of early attachment classifications may lie in the internal working model mechanism. Internal models are not just "pictures" but refer to the feelings aroused. They enable a person to anticipate and interpret another's behavior and plan a response. If an infant experiences their caregiver as a source of security and support, they are more likely to develop a positive self-image and expect positive reactions from others. Conversely, a child from an abusive relationship with the caregiver may internalize a negative self-image and generalize negative expectations into other relationships. The internal working models on which attachment behavior is based show a degree of continuity and stability. Children are likely to fall into the same categories as their primary caregivers indicating that the caregivers' internal working models affect the way they relate to their child. This effect has been observed to continue across three generations. Bowlby believed that the earliest models formed were the most likely to persist because they existed in the subconscious. Such models are not, however, impervious to change given further relationship experiences; a minority of children have different attachment classifications with different caregivers.

There is some evidence that gender differences in attachment patterns of adaptive significance begin to emerge in middle childhood. Insecure attachment and early psychosocial stress indicate the presence of environmental risk (for example poverty, mental illness, instability, minority status, violence). This can tend to favor the development of strategies for earlier reproduction. However, different patterns have different adaptive values for males and females. Insecure males tend to adopt avoidant strategies, whereas insecure females tend to adopt anxious/

ambivalent strategies, unless they are in a very high-risk environment. Adrenarche is proposed as the endocrine mechanism underlying the reorganization of insecure attachment in middle childhood.

Attachment in Adults:

Attachment theory was extended to adult romantic relationships in the late 1980s by Cindy Hazan and Phillip Shaver.

Four styles of attachment have been identified in adults:

- secure,
- anxious-preoccupied,
- dismissive-avoidant
- Fearful-avoidant.

These roughly correspond to infant classifications: secure, insecure-ambivalent, insecure-avoidant and disorganized/disoriented.

1. **Securely attached adults** tend to have positive views of themselves, their partners and their relationships. They feel comfortable with intimacy and independence, balancing the two. Anxious-preoccupied adults seek high levels of intimacy, approval and responsiveness from partners, becoming overly dependent. They tend to be less trusting, have less positive views about themselves and their partners, and may exhibit high levels of emotional expressiveness, worry and impulsiveness in their relationships.

2. **Anxious preoccupied adults** desire a high level of independence, often appearing to avoid attachment altogether. They view themselves as self-sufficient, invulnerable to attachment feelings and not needing close relationships. They tend to suppress their feelings, dealing with rejection by distancing themselves from partners of whom they often have a poor opinion.

3. **Dismissive-avoidant adults** have mixed feelings about close relationships, both desiring and feeling uncomfortable with emotional closeness. They tend to mistrust their partners and view themselves as unworthy.

4. Like dismissive-avoidant adults, **fearful-avoidant adults** tend to seek less intimacy, suppressing their feelings.

The point of the classical theorists is not only do biological and genetic individual differences in development exist in children; but also, that there are outside factors such as parental interaction, environmental exposure, etc. that can have a profound influence on children's' developmental patterns.

MODULE 4

The Family Life Cycle

THE FAMILY LIFE CYCLE

Clusters of Problems:
- Normal Stage specific difficulties
- Maladaptive responses to the specific pressures of a given stage
- Chronic problems related to unresolved issues from a prior developmental stage or stages

Two Kinds of Stressors in Families:
- **Horizontal Stressors:**

  These stressors correspond to the crises associated with the family's movement through the life cycle.

  Ex. Birth of a child, Accidental death of a child, Teenager gets pregnant

- **Vertical Stressors:**

  These stressors include patterns of relating and functioning that are transmitted across generations.

  Ex. The legacies and missions handed down through the generations

Changes Occur at Different Levels:
- Changes at the Individual Level
- Changes at the Systemic Level
- Changes at the Relational Ethics Level

Theorists:
- **Individual Theorists**
  - Freud-Psychosexual Development
  - Erikson-Psychosocial Development
  - Piaget-Cognitive Development
  - Kohlberg-Moral Development

- **Couple Theorists**
  - ○ Hendrix
  - ○ Gottmann
  - ○ Scharf & Scharf

- **Family Theorists**
  - ○ Minuchin
  - ○ Bowen
  - ○ Haley
  - ○ White
  - ○ DeShazer

STAGE I
THE FAMILY LIFE CYCLE
MARRIAGE

- Two separate individuals must establish a new unit consisting of the couple. As they come together, they must establish reasonable boundaries with their families of origin.

The Major Tasks at This Stage are related to both partner's moving away from families of origin and toward one another.

- **Lewis believes there are three stages:**
    o Initial Stages is when similarities and rapport are explored.
    o Intermediate Stages are when mutual self-disclosure and empathy occur.
    o Later Stages is when there is a solid dyad.

- **Social Exchange Theories**
    o These theories were developed by Blau and Homans in the 50s and 60s.

o These theorists emphasize an economic metaphor that views relationships as extended markets. Individuals are self-interested and trying to maximize wins and decrease losses.

o Interdependence though is important in terms of this theory because each person's happiness depends on the other person's happiness. A high degree of interdependence is achieved when one partner realizes that his or her happiness is maximized when the partner's happiness is maximized. It benefits the self.

o Rewards refer to the benefits exchanged in social relationships, and are defined as the pleasures, satisfactions, and gratifications a person derives from participating in a relationship.

o Costs refer to the drawbacks or expenses associated with a particular relationship.

o Comparison levels refer to the unique values and expectations individuals bring into the relationship. These are the standards upon which the relationship is judges.

o Comparison levels are influenced by a person's family of origin, information gained from observing peer relationships, and the individual's own experiences in relationships.

THINKING QUESTION:

Getting Married:

People say that marriage ruins a good sex life. In your opinion, is this true or not true and why? Think about the pluses and minuses involved in the institution of marriage.

Moving Beyond Attraction:

- **Trust, Commitment, and Relationship Turning Points**
  - o Trust refers to the belief that one's partner will not exploit or take unfair advantage of his or her.
  - o Commitment is reflected in the degree to which we are willing to work for the continuation of the relationship, and it is in this willingness to work for the relationship that distinguishes an increasingly intimate and exclusive relationship from one that is casual and unchanging.
  - o Turning Points. A relationship goes through critical periods or turning points. This is when a relationship either evolves to a deeper level of intimacy and involvement or dissolves.

- **Attachment Theory:**
  - o Attachment Theory (Bowlby-see earlier) implies that the capacity to form emotional attachments to others is primarily developed during infancy and early childhood.
  - o Infants experience less anxiety when their caretakers are in close proximity. This elicits feelings of security and love for the child.
  - o If the child does not experience adequate attention from caregivers, he or she may become less self-assured and less trusting of them and be at risk for developing insecure attachment relationships.
  - o The primary emotional experiences that children have with parents and caretakers form the basis of what Bowlby calls the internal working model.
  - o A child's internal working model assumes that expectations, beliefs, feelings, that an individual develops, because of the responsiveness of caregivers, are later transferred to, and displayed in, other close relationships.

- **Three Distinct Attachment Patterns:**
  - o **Secure**-when parents are responsive to a child, the child will become securely attached and be less inhibitive and exhibit more exploratory behavior.
  - o **Avoidant**- Constantly ignoring or deflecting the needs and the attention of the child leads to Avoidant Attachment style in which the child attempts to maintain proximity but avoids close contact with the caregiver.
  - o **Anxious**-Ambivalent- When a parent is inconsistent in responding and attention giving, the child has an anxious ambivalent attachment that tries to re-establish contact, clings to the caregiver, and constantly looks to see where the caregiver is.

- **At the Individual Level**:
  - Both partners have to look less to their families of origin and more toward each other for meeting basic emotional needs such as caring, comfort, company, and support.

- **Developmental Tasks of the Married Couple Include:**
  - Establishing an Identity as a Married Couple.
  - Establishing Marital Themes
  - Negotiating Marital Roles
  - Evolving a Congruence of Conjugal Identities
  - Regulating Distances Between Family and Friends
  - Managing the Household
  - Managing the Emotional Climate of the Relationship
  - Evolving a Marital Sexual Script
  - Managing Conflict

- **At the Systemic Level:**
  - Both partners have to establish a series of ground rules and patterns that allow them to function well as a couple.

- **At the Relational Ethical Level:**
  - The central task involves both partners' efforts to balance loyalties to their families of origin, their new partners and themselves.

- **Gay and Lesbian Marriage**

o It is estimated that 1% of adult women self-identify as lesbian and 2% of men identify as gay.

o It is estimated that 50% of gay women and 40% of gay men between the ages of 18-59 are currently living with a same sex partner.

o 60% of heterosexuals are living with a partner.

o The experience of these couples is more similar than different to heterosexual couples.

- **Typical Problems at This Stage Include:**
  o Chronic Arguing
  o Constant tension and "walking on eggshells."
  o Difficulties setting ground rules or resolving conflicts.
  o Complaints of selfishness, unavailability, or demanding
  o Having a hard time balancing loyalties between family of origin and marital relationship. "I'm going home to mother" syndrome.
  o Family Cutoffs. Cutting off family of origin. This is also a problem of boundaries.

- **THINKING QUESTION:**

Mate Section:

Theorists have different opinions regarding mate selection: Basically they hold two opposite views: birds of a feather flock together or opposites attract. In your opinion, which do you believe is the case and why?

Couples therapists believe that when a couple come together they "know" right away whether there is a "click" or not. They also believe that this click is an unconscious recognition that this person is a "soulmate." There is some anecdotal evidence that suggests this might be the case in that if you ask married couples how they knew this was the person they wanted to marry, they say, "I just knew." I had one husband say to me, "As soon as I saw her, I knew I would marry her. I didn't care if she was an ax murderer, I knew we would be together!" In your opinion, discuss why or why not this theory is true and why.

STAGE II

BIRTH OF THE CHILDREN

The birth of children has a sweeping impact on the lives of the two new parents.

The major task is to attempt to integrate their relationship that already exists between the two of them. They have to integrate the parental subsystem into the couple.

Other Developmental Tasks Accompanying Parenthood:
- Altering Family Themes
- Defining a Parental Role Identity
- The Child's Evolving Identity
- Renegotiating Distances With Family and Friends
- Realigning Marital Boundaries
- Balancing the Boundary Between Work and Family
- Making a Family Household
- Managing Finances

- Maintaining the Couple Relationship
- Maintaining a Satisfying Sexual Relationship
- Managing Leisure Activities
- Managing New Areas of Conflict

At the Individual Level:
- Increased Level of Physical and Emotional Demands Placed on Two People
- Responsibility for Caring for the New Baby
- New Skills are Needed
- Individual Identities are Changed:
  - Positive- New Meaning to Life
  - Negative- Parents Feel Inadequate

At the Systemic Level:
- This means the creation of new boundaries, subsystems and roles.
- The marital subsystem must make room for the parental subsystem.
- The boundaries they create will regulate the coexistence of these subsystems within the new family. Ex. Child having his or her own room.

At the Relational Ethics Level:

- The basic task involves both parents' efforts to balance their increasingly complex networks of obligation and entitlement—at this point, obligations to one's child, one's spouse, one's family of origin and one's self.

Typical Problems:

One is overinvolved with the child

Decreased marital satisfaction

Depressed and/or overwhelmed

Insufficient involvement with the child

Intense, stormy marital relationship

THINKING QUESTION:

Marriage and Young Children:

And baby makes three. First the first time, there is a triangle. Becoming a couple and becoming parents are the activities of people in their twenties and thirties. The trap here is that the couple loses the couple and they start relating to each other as parents and nothing more. What precautions can couples take to safeguard against this?

THINKING QUESTION:

Divorce:

Some people say that Divorce should be a stage in the "normal" life cycle because the majority of people get divorced in US society (57% in NYS). Do you agree or disagree with this statement? If you choose at some point in your life to divorce, what protections can you make for yourself and/or your children?

STAGE III

ELEMENTARY SCHOOL

Individuation of the Children

This stage starts when the child is two.

There are two aspects:
- Beginning social activity outside the home, with peers and adults, at school or play.
- Involves natural evolution of parental expectations regarding the child, which coincides with the child's developing readiness for such expectations.

The Major Tasks are Twofold:
- Trying to balance the growing autonomy of the child with his or her sense of belonging and loyalty to the family, without either "binding" or "expelling" the child.
- Trying to maintain a reasonable and fair balance of accountability between parents and child, without either overburdening the child with expectations and missions or expecting too little or nothing of the child.

The Individual Level:

- Parents must face what may be their first sense of psychological separation from the child.
- They may experience increased fears concerning the child's welfare out of the house, out of sight, as well as concern over the kinds of influence to which the child will be exposed.
- The child may face fears associated with the world outside or fears of being separated from parents, etc.
- The child has to begin to consider how to balance his or her own needs and desires with those of other children as well as with their parents.
- The child begins to develop a need and capacity to contribute, to be of help in some way, especially to his or her parents and other family members.

The Systemic Level:

- The boundaries between and around the child and the parents are significantly changed at this point.
- The child becomes involved in systems outside the family, such as friendships with peers and school.
- The child begins to spend more time away from home and parents.
- The boundaries between child and parents become firmer than they previously have been.
- The clarity and flexibility of these boundaries between these systems become increasingly important as the child grows older.
- If there are two or more children, the sibling subsystem is created.
- As the children become less involved with parents, the necessity of maintaining boundaries between generations and of balancing marital and parental obligations continues.

The Relational Ethical Level:

- The child may begin to take on missions and with them roles which can exert a major influence on his or future life.
- These could be missions to care for one or both parents for their marriage, for the family as a whole or to achieve and reflect

pride toward the family. All these may become noticeable at this time.

- These missions may or may not be harmful to the child depending on the flexibility of the parents.

- **Questions for Parents to Explore:**
  - Is too much being asked of the child?
  - Is the child being asked to put aside their own needs in order to help others in the family?
  - Is merit of the child's contributions being acknowledged?
  - Is too little being expected of the child?
  - Does the child contribute anything?
  - Does she give too much, too little?

- **Four Parenting Styles:**
  - o **The Indulgent Parents:**
    - ▪ Indulgent Parents are referred to as permissive or non-directive, as responsive but not demanding. They avoid confrontation.
      - • **Two Types:**
        - o **Democratic** are more conscientious, engaged, and committed to the children
        - o **Non-Directive** Parents are much more laid back in their approach.

  - o **The Authoritarian Parents:**
    - ▪ Authoritarian parents are highly demanding and directive, but not responsive. They are obedience and status oriented and expect their orders to be obeyed without explanation. These parents want to curb the child's self-will. They use punitive and forceful methods to accomplish this.
  - o **The Authoritative Parents:**
    - ▪ The Authoritative Parents are both demanding and responsive. They impart clear standards for their children and are assertive but nor intrusive and restrictive.

- o **The Uninvolved Parents:**
  - Uninvolved parents are low I both responsiveness and demandingness. These parents can be thought of as both neglectful and permissive. Children are given no clear rules for behavior and they receive little or no attention. This type of parenting can leave children anxious, confused, and unable to internalize standards for self-control.
- o **Common Problems:**

  - Families having problems at this stage usually present the child in therapy as the identified patient.
  - The one exception is the single parent who presents with depression, anxiety, loneliness, when the child starts school. Very often she feels unemployed.
  - Usually though the problem is defined as relational, that is, they define it as a problem between parents and child.
  - **School Phobia.** It is common for the child to want to stay home or not want to go to school. Here the child could be afraid of school or what is called a fear could reflect loyalty and responsibility on the part of the child for the parent in the home. It could also reflect the family member not being able to tolerate the absence of the child.
  - Child could have **enuresis** and/or **encopresis**.

- Child could refuse to be separated from her doll.
- Child could develop a psychosomatic disorder such as asthma or stomach aches.
- Child may act stubborn, rebellious, or selfish.
- Child may have **temper tantrums**. This usually reflects a child who is not held accountable enough by parents. It could also reflect a child whom little is expected by parents, much is allowed, and discipline is inconsistent or near existent.

- These children are paradoxically deprived. They are deprived of learning about those aspects of reality such as needs, feelings, and rights of others, which would result in the child to put limits on their own behaviors, needs and expectations. Without any effective counterbalance, these needs go unchecked.
- The result is that the natural limitations may begin to feel unreasonable to these children.

NOTES:

STAGE IV

INDIVIDUATION OF THE ADOLESCENTS

The Wonder Years

- Puberty signals the beginning of this stage.
- Physical and psychological changes disrupt structural patterns that had evolved between the parent and the child.
- Central task for the family is to redefine the terms of the parent- child relationship. This is primarily regarding issues of autonomy, responsibility, and control without fundamentally violating their basic trustworthiness.
- The child is in limbo-- not a child, not an adult.

The Individual Psychological Level
- Parents face a loss of control over the now adolescent son/ daughter.
- Parents may be faced for the first time with overt rebellion.
- Parents are confronted with the child's development of sexual maturity.
- Parents may feel as though they are losing their child.
- For the teenagers, there is a loss of play.
- There is a loss of special exemptions because they are children.
- They are confronted with the tasks of adulthood.
- There are increased responsibilities.
- They are expected to work- to get a driver's license.
- There are issues of sexuality, identity, and peer group relations.

The Systemic Level

- Fundamental change involves strengthening of boundaries between parents and adolescents.
- Clearly expressed in adolescent's room.
- Teenager's participation in the system of the family begins to be more evenly balanced by participation in the system of peers outside the home.

The Relational Ethical Level

- As the teenager begins to develop a more separate autonomous self apart from the family, she necessarily becomes more involved in developing his other identity as a separate, individual person.
- The efforts to balance loyalties to self and to others in the family necessarily become complex.
- Parents may feel underappreciated or shortchanged. Parents may experience doubts about trusting adolescents.
- From the adolescent side, trust of parents is often endangered by the imposition of parental decisions or rules.
- The parents may feel ambivalent. Parents are torn between the urge to hold onto the child and to see him or her group and away. Similarly, the adolescent may be torn between urges to grow out of the family and to remain in it as a child.

- The adolescent may begin to take on certain missions of the family. These are important that they may influence what Erikson has called the search for identity.
- Teen may feel expected to carry on the family traditions. May bear a strong legacy to achieve or succeed in some way to reflect pride on family or the opposite, to fail so as not to surpass a parent's level of achievement.

Common Problems:
- Rebellious acting out adolescent, such as poor grades in school, truancy, experiencing with drugs, running away from home.
- The second problem usually involves not the adolescent who is struggling for freedom but the opposite case-- one who is tied to parents.

Individuation
- It is important for the young adults to feel psychologically free from their parent's control.
- It is crucially important for parent's to work as a team during this stage--to be on the same page.

Main Task is to safely create a departure from the home

THINKING QUESTION:

Parents of Teenagers:

One of my clients said that living with teenagers was like oral surgery without Novocain, like a thousand paper cuts or like Debby Boone singing "You light up my life" over and over. (You-tube her). What did he mean by this? Are there issues that arise that are unique for parents of teenagers? What are they? How can teenagers bring joy to a marriage? Stress to a marriage? What were the issues you faced when you were a teenager?

STAGE V

DEPARTURE OF THE CHILDREN

The main task is to separate without breaking ties.
Families need to balance a dual commitment.

The Individual Psychological Level
- Parents are faced with the loss of the child as a focus in their daily lives.
- **The Empty Nest Syndrome**
  o In most families there is some sort of preparation since the child has been growing more independent.
- The young person may face unfamiliarity of living alone, loneliness or homesickness and/or a sense of not fitting in.
- They are forced to accept responsibility

The Systemic Level
- Departure of the child involves a major change in the boundaries within the family.
- Change in the physical boundaries occurs- - the child is outside of the home.

- When the child develops a couple's relationship, there is another change in the structure to accommodate the "in-law."
- If there are any younger children at home, they get promoted to the rank of oldest child.

Three Modes of Separation between Parents and Adolescents
- **The Binding Mode**
  - Here the child is unable to leave home. These bound young adults remain in the house, often out of a mixture of concerns for and an attachment to the family and fears of facing stressful aspects of independent living.
- **The Delegating Mode**
  - Here the child is sent out of the family but with some kind of mission to accomplish. They are permitted to leave home but they are held responsible by themselves as well as others in the family to pursue the missions called for by the family structure and history.
- **The Expelling Mode**
  - Here the child is spit out of the family with no missions to fulfill. They are permitted to leave, forced to leave with little sense that they are either wanted or needed by the family.

The Relational Ethics Level
- Does the child have a right to leave home?
- Is the child entitled to have a life of his or her own?
- Like the young adult, parents are trying to balance their dual commitments to the grown child, to themselves, and to each other.
- The parent child relationship at this point clearly becomes a two way street.

Common Problems:
- Exaggeration of some aspect of the separation process.
  - Some adult children remain at home indefinitely.
  - Some adult children are kicked out of the house.

- o The young adult repeatedly fails to live alone.
- o Feelings of isolation--not fitting in new job--anxiety, despair.
- • Marital complaints
- • As with each of the earlier stages, the poorer the resolution of an earlier stage, the more difficult the tasks of the following stage will become. The better the resolution of this particular stage, the better prepared the family will be for the last stage.

THINKING QUESTION:

The Quarter life Crisis:
Discuss what you see as contributing to the Quarter life Crisis. The quarter life crisis refers to what seems to be the mini crises occurring in 20 somethings. I have posted an article I wrote that explains it in more detail. Think about this crisis from a social and historical framework. Present personal information (from acquaintances/friends/relatives or yourself if you choose) that you have heard or observed that relates to this new phenomenon.

THINKING QUESTION:

Menopause:
Hot flashes, depression, homicidal and suicidal feelings—these are but a few of the symptoms that young women are taught about menopause. Are they true—not true? Can they be compared to PMS? Is there such a thing as PMS? What are the effects? How do you think these life cycle events affect relationships? There is a paper posted regarding this topic as well (http://www.NYMFT.Com.

THINKING QUESTION:

Late Adulthood:

Some people say they have abandonment fears; some people say they have abandonment fantasies. What does this refer to, in your opinion?

NOTES:

STAGE VI

AGING AND DEATH OF THE PARENTS

The basic task involves facing and accepting a variety of losses.

The family's task is to face and accept these losses without significantly damaging the basic level of trustworthiness, which has been built up in these relationships.

Losses:

- **Relational Losses.** There are the parent's losses of friends, the survivor's loss of a spouse, and the children's loss of parents.
- **Physical Losses.** There are possible health losses as person's age, vocational losses in retirement and possibly financial losses.

The Individual Psychological Level
- If not working, the individual may feel some loss of self-esteem, self-worth.
- They may feel as though they are no longer making a contribution.
- They may miss the activity, the social life.
- They may feel unwanted-- as though they have been put out to pasture.
- As old age progresses, they must cope with a gradual diminishing of physical strength. They may have difficulty hearing, seeing, etc.
- These physical losses may affect a person's ego integrity.
- Each person faces his or her own death, his or her own accomplishments, failures, regrets, and satisfactions. They might experience increased stress, irritability. They may complain.
- As old age progresses, they must cope with a gradual diminishing of physical strength. They may have difficulty hearing, seeing, etc.

- These physical losses may affect a person's ego integrity.
- Each person faces his or her own death, his or her own accomplishments, failures, regrets, and satisfactions.
- They might experience increased stress, irritability. They may complain.

The Systemic Level

- The adult child and the parent may become afraid.

THINKING QUESTION:

The Sandwich Generation:

I was food shopping the other day and in produce I overheard two women talking. They were talking about vacations with one off them saying she was so happy to be finally going on vacation and she was so happy she found a competent sitter. I assumed they were discussing their children. They weren't! They were discussing getting a sitter for their older parents who lived with them while they went on vacation.

The sandwich generation refers to people in their fifties who may still have children at home and who also have a parent living with them who possibly needs care-taking because of ill health. In 2 pages, discuss the issues that could arise in such a situation. How would you go about solving them?

The Relational Ethical Level

- Both the dying person and the survivor may ask themselves if they did enough for each other.
- They may wish that they had done more or that they could undo certain things.
- They may wish that they could make up for certain things.
- They may ask for forgiveness.
- It is important that the adult children beguiled by some notion of realistic accountability in weighing how much they can give and in what ways.

Common Problems

- If the parent is ill, the spouse may present with symptoms of anxiety and/or depression.
- If the parent dies, there is a grief reaction for the adult child.
- If the spouse dies, there is a grief reaction for the missed partner.
- If the parent lives with the adult child, either can present with complaints.
- The spouse of the adult child may have complaints.
- A couple who have regulated distance in the marriage by triangulating in the parent may need to substitute a different third party (a lover, a child, a bottle, a therapist

THINKING QUESTIONS:

Challenges of Growing Older:

The challenges that face older people are many in this society. There is much talk about elder abuse, drug abuse in elders, neglect and many other issues as well. Think about these issues and speculate on solutions to these social problems.

THINKING QUESTION:

Valuing Older Adults:
In this society we do not value older adults. Why is that? Can you envision a society where age is valued and older people are considered wise? What would have to be different about our society in order for us to experience wisdom in our older people?

THINKING QUESTION:

The End of Life:
Think about the quality vs the quantity of life. Think how the decline of health affects the psychology of quality of life in older people.

THINKING QUESTION:

The End of Life

Is there such a thing as The Good Death? What factors do you think are involved in creating an environment conducive for the Good Death to occur? Are there any?

Kubler Ross, who has written extensively in the process of dying, has probably done the most research on how people die. She presented five stages of dying: denial, anger, bargaining, depression, and acceptance.

Think about examples of each stage.

What are the challenges faced by older people, such as mental illness, alcohol and drug abuse, dementia, victimization, elder abuse, sexual issues etc. What do you see as some solutions to these Issues?

MODULE 5

Building Positive Relations with your Children

OBJECTIVES:

This next section will enable the parents in your group become more aware of their family in general, their emotions, family atmosphere, family values, and their family lifestyle. In addition, the parents will explore the sex roles. They will learn about the basic skills for building position relationships with their children. They will also explore the goals of misbehavior and positive behavior.

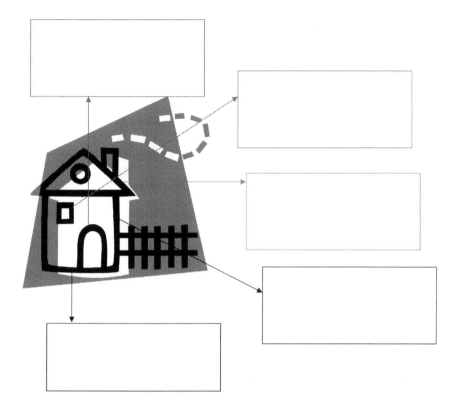

BUILDING MY HOME

✓ The foundation: Write the beliefs that govern your life.
✓ The walls: Write methods you use to strengthen these beliefs in your family.
✓ The roof: How do you protect or defend you values?
✓ The window: Write something about your family values that you are proud of.
✓ The door: If someone entered your home, what would they notice that gives them clues about your values?

PERSONAL DEVELOPMENT EXERCISE

ENCOURAGEMENT:

1. Take an inventory of your assets: What are the things you like about the way you relate with your child/children. Recognize positive aspects of the relationship. List at least five things.

2. How can you use these assets to further improve the way you relate to your child/children?

3. What are the things you like about your child/children? Recognize positive traits and consider alternatives to what may appear to be negative traits. List at least five things.

4. How can you focus on these assets and become a more encouraging parent? Make some specific plans

UNDERSTANDING MORE ABOUT YOUR CHILD AND ABOUT YOURSELF AS A PARENT

EMOTIONS:

Typically, we regard emotions as magical forces that invade us from the outside. We seem not to realize that each of us is responsible for her or his own emotions. Our emotions are based on our beliefs and purposes. ***We feel as we believe.***

Parents often become annoyed and angry with children because the children will not do what the parents want them to. These hostile feelings of anger and annoyance serve the purpose of controlling the children. Once parents decide that they do not need to be controlling (that they can set limits and let the children decide and learn from the consequences), then there is no purpose for becoming annoyed and angry.

Children learn to use their emotions to achieve goals as well. Once parents recognize how children can use emotions to achieve goals, parents are in a position to influence their children. We know that becoming responsible for one's own feelings is a necessary part of growing—and becoming an effective parent.

UNDERSTANDING MORE ABOUT YOUR CHILD
AND YOURSELF AS A PARENT (Cont.)

LIFESTYLE:

We develop beliefs about who we are, who and what other people are, what is important in life, and how we should function so that we can belong. We live by our beliefs; they characterize our *lifestyle*.

Yet, our basic beliefs are often faulty. Why? Because our interpretations of our experiences are often inaccurate. We formed our most basic beliefs when we were very young. At that time our limited experience caused us to misjudge and overgeneralize.

It is important to understand the factors that influence the formation of our children's lifestyle. The four major factors that contribute to the formation of the children's lifestyle are:

- *Family atmosphere and values:*

  The patterns in the human relationships set by parents are called the "family atmosphere." The atmosphere may be:

  - Competitive or cooperative
  - Friendly or hostile
  - Autocratic or permissive
  - Orderly or chaotic

- *Family values:*

  Family values can be easily recognizable (valuing religion, education, hard work), while others may not be as obvious (valuing power, control, winning, being right). Share interests reflect the family values. Children cannot remain neutral about the values their family holds. Each child must decide which and how much of the values of the family to adopt as their own.

- *Sex roles:*

The sex roles played by parents are guidelines for their children. Children base their attitudes toward their own sex and the opposite sex on their observations of their parents. They may accept or reject the models their parents present.

- *Birth order:*

The psychological position of a child in a family is often related to the child's position among siblings. Each child has a different position in the family and perceives all events from her or his own viewpoint. Each position tends to have its own characteristic line of development and related beliefs and attitudes. It is important to recognize that these positions in the family constellation only influence an individual's personality development; they do not directly determine it. Each individual makes his or her own decisions.

- *Methods of training:*

Parents' attitudes and behavior toward children and toward themselves influences children's lifestyle. A parent may be autocratic or permissive or inconsistent in their behavior towards their children, and this is greatly influenced by how they were reared. A parent's lifestyle growing up influences his or her present behavior as parents. However, the results of our training are not always what we expect, because it is the child, not the parents, who decides how the child will respond.

It is in response to these four major influences (family atmosphere and values, sex roles, birth order, and methods of training) that children develop their convictions and long-range goals. If they are able to meet their immediate goals through constructive acts, they become cooperative children. If, however, they find that they cannot achieve their goals constructively, they may become discouraged children who feel they must misbehave to secure a place in life.

THE FOUR BASIC INGREDIENTS FOR BUILDING POSITIVE RELATIONSHIPS

1. *MUTUAL RESPECT:*

   Respect is earned; it comes from showing respect to others. To establish mutual respect, we must be willing to demonstrate respect for our children.

   ✓ Minimize negative talk.
   ✓ Talk with your children when the atmosphere is calm.

2. *ENCOURAGEMENT:*

   We must believe in our children if they are to believe in themselves.

   ✓ Minimize the importance of your children's mistakes.
   ✓ Recognize their assets and strengths.

3. *COMMUNICATING LOVE:*

   To feel secure, each child must have at least one significant person to love and to be loved by.

✓ Tell your children you love them when they are not anticipating it.
✓ Nonverbal signs such as pats, hugs, kisses, and tousling hair are extremely important.

4. *SPENDING TIME TOGETHER:*

The important ingredient of time together is *quality* not quantity. An hour of positive relationship is worth more than several hours of conflict.

✓ Spend time each day with each child doing something you **both** enjoy.
✓ Agree on the time. Plan the activity together. Do not allow interruptions.
✓ Keep it simple. Keep it consistent. Follow through.

UNDERSTANDING BEHAVIOR

Behavior occurs for a social purpose. People are decision-making social beings whose main goal in life is to belong. In our search, we select beliefs, feelings and behavior that we feel will gain us significance. Behavior can best be understood by observing its consequences.

✓ Observe your own reaction to the child's misbehavior. *Your feelings* point to the child's goals.
✓ Observe the child's response to your attempts at correction. *The child's response to your behavior* will also let you know what the child is after.
✓ Train yourself to look at the results of misbehavior rather than just at the misbehavior.
✓ The results of the misbehavior reveal its purpose.

All misbehavior stems from discouragement. The child lacks the courage to behave in an active, constructive manner. A child may use misbehavior for different goals or misbehave in different ways to achieve the same purpose.

NOTE: Children are often aware of the consequences of their misbehavior, but they are usually unaware of their goals.

Points to remember when trying to understand behavior:

✓ Effective parenting requires patience.
✓ Effective parenting requires active attendance and awareness.
✓ All behavior has a social purpose.
✓ Responsible children are influenced by responsible parents.
✓ Focus on the child's assets and strength, rather than on finding fault.
✓ Showing confidence in the child will help the child develop self-confidence.

NOTES:

THE FOUR GOALS OF MISBEHAVIOR

ATTENTION:

Children prefer to gain attention through useful ways but will seek attention in useless ways if that is the only way they can get attention. Children who hold the conviction that they can belong only if they are receiving attention prefer negative attention to being ignored.

- ✓ Focus on constructive behavior.
- ✓ Ignore misbehavior or pay attention to it in ways the child does not expect.
- ✓ Attention should not be given on demand, even for positive acts.
- ✓ Give attention when it is not expected. This changes the emphasis from 'getting attention' to being 'given attention.'

POWER:

Power-seeking children feel they are significant only when they are boss. Some children in power struggles do what they are told, but not in a way the parents want it done (defiant compliance).

- ✓ Refrain from getting angry.
- ✓ Disengage from the power struggle.
- ✓ Do not use power tactics to counter children's bids for power. This only impresses them with the value of power and increases their desire for it.

REVENGE:

Children who pursue revenge believe they are significant only when they are hurting others, as they believe they have been hurt. They find a place by being cruel and disliked.

✓ Do not retaliate.
✓ Remain calm and show good will.

DISPLAY OF INADEQUACY:

Children, who display inadequacy, or disability, are *extremely* discouraged. They have given up hope of succeeding. They attempt to keep others from expecting anything of them. Giving up may be total or only in areas where children feel they can't succeed.

✓ Eliminate all criticism.
✓ Focus on the child's assets and strengths.
✓ Encourage any effort to improve, no matter how small it seems.

Points to remember when trying to understand behavior:

✓ Your reactions and feelings about a child's misbehavior point to the purpose of that behavior.
✓ Changing your own behavior can most effectively influence the child's behavior.
✓ When the child is misbehaving, do what he or she does not expect, that is consider doing exactly the opposite from what you would typically do.
✓ Show appreciation for the child's positive behaviors, unless they are meant only to gain attention.
✓ Withdraw from power struggles.
✓ Because retaliation stimulates further revenge, do not retaliate. Express good will to improve the quality of the relationship.

✓ A child who seeks power often has a parent who likes to boss others.

✓ A child who displays inadequacy is not unable; rather, the child lacks belief in his or her ability.

Positive Interaction Loop

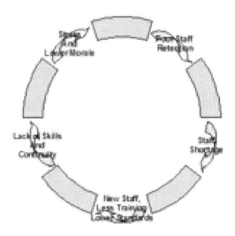

GOALS OF POSITIVE BEHAVIOR

ATTENTION/INVOLVEMENT/CONTRIBUTION:

- Child's belief: "I belong by contributing."
- Behavior: Helps. Volunteers.
- How to encourage positive goals: Let child know the contribution counts and that you appreciate it.

POWER/AUTONOMY/RESPONSIBILITY FOR OWN BEHAVIOR:

- Child's belief: "I can decide and be responsible for my behavior."
- Behavior: Shows self-discipline. Does own work. Is resourceful.
- How to encourage positive goals: Encourage child's decision making. Let child experience both positive and negative outcomes. Express confidence in child.

JUSTICE/FAIRNESS:

- Child's belief: "I am interested in cooperating."
- Behavior: Returns kindness for hurt. Ignores belittling comments.
- How to encourage positive goals: Let child know you appreciate her or his interest in cooperating.

WITHDRAWAL FROM CONFLICT-REFUSAL TO FIGHT-ACCEPTANCE OF OTHERS' OPINIONS:

- Child's belief: "I can decide to withdraw from conflict."
- Behavior: Ignores provocations. Withdraws from power contest to decide own behavior.
- How to encourage positive goals: Recognize child's effort to act maturely.

POINTS TO REMEMBER:

Temperament and the Developmental Stages of Children

1. Each child is born with an individual temperament. Accept a child's temperament and build on it.
2. Each child goes through stages of development at an individual rate and in a particular style.
3. Each developmental stage has proposed tasks that children master when they are ready. For example:
   - ✓ Infant: task is to learn to trust other humans, themselves, and the world around them
   - ✓ Toddler: task is to experiment with independence
   - ✓ Preschooler: tasks are to create their own worlds, practice adult roles, play with language, and learn to get along with other children

4. Children often sense parents' expectations of them and react as expected.
5. To enhance parenting, find and create opportunities to say *"yes"* rather than "NO."
6. Help children to respect themselves and others. Encouraging children's positive beliefs about themselves can lead to positive behavior patterns.
7. Allow children time to play. Play is their work, and they must do it to develop and grow.
8. Provide freedom within limits. A democratic family atmosphere builds responsibility and teaches children respect for themselves and others.

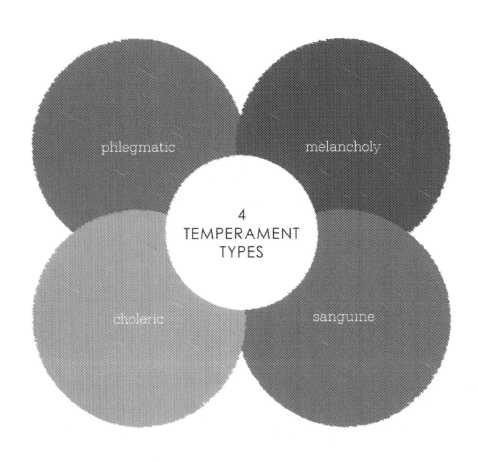

phlegmatic

melancholy

4
TEMPERAMENT
TYPES

choleric

sanguine

ENCOURAGEMENT

A WAY TO DEVELOP A CHILD'S POTENTIAL

The language of encouragement avoids value judgments by eliminating words like good, great and terrific. Instead, it focuses on the individual's strengths, conveys a message of confidence in the individual, and helps promote high self-esteem.

Phrases that demonstrate acceptance:

"I like the way you handled that."
"I'm glad you enjoyed yourself."
"How do you feel about this?"

Phrases that show confidence:

"You'll make it."
"You're making progress."
"I believe you'll handle it."

Phrases that recognize effort and improvement:

"I can see you put a lot of effort into that."
"I can see a lot of progress."
"You're improving in _____."

Strategies for Encouraging:

1. Give responsibility.
2. Show appreciation for efforts made to help the household function smoothly.
3. Ask for opinions and suggestions.
4. Encourage participation in decision-making.
5. Accept mistakes
6. Emphasize the process, not the product.

7. Focus on the child's strengths and assets, not on his or her faults.
8. Show confidence in your child's judgment.
9. Have positive expectations.
10. Develop alternative ways of viewing situations.

Encouragement, Self-Worth and Self Esteem are examined more thoroughly in a later chapter.

NOTES:

THE RIGHTS OF PARENTS AND CHILDREN

Oftentimes parents may see themselves as all sacrificing for their children. This attitude is stressful for parents and unhealthy for children. Children who grow up feeling they have to be the center of the universe may have problems in relationships. Consider the rights listed below. They can be summed up in one phrase: the right to mutual respect.

Parents have the right to:

✓ Live their lives apart from their children.
✓ Time for themselves and adult relationships.
✓ Friendships with others.
✓ Privacy.
✓ Have their property respected.

Children have the right to:

✓ Be raised in a loving, safe atmosphere.
✓ Have their wishes considered.
✓ Be respected as a unique individual.
✓ A life apart from being the child in the family.
✓ Privacy.
✓ Have their property respected.

What will you do this week to maintain your rights?

How will you show respect for your child's rights?

MODULE 6

Developing Effective Communication Skills

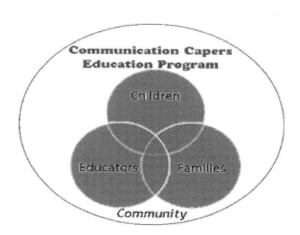

EARLY CHILD
COMMUNICATION STYLES

Your ten-year-old daughter says to you, "I don't know what's wrong with me. Ginny used to like me, but now she doesn't. She never comes to our house to play and when I go to hers she always plays with Joyce and the two of them play together and have fun and ignore me. I just stand there all by myself. I hate them both."

Which of the following best describes how you would react?

a) Well who would want to play with you? I told you to care about how you look.

b) It's OK honey, I'll play with you, what would you like to do?

c) Why don't you ask both Ginny and Joyce to play here?

d) You're just jealous of Ginny.

e) Come on—let's talk about something more pleasant.

f) Do the kids ever tell you why they don't want to play with you?

g) Other:_____

You receive a note home that your twelve-year-old son was throwing things and being disruptive in school. He says, "I didn't do anything! The teacher is always picking on me. He hates me!"

Which of the following best describes how you would react?

a) Go for the aspirins.

b) I don't blame the teacher for picking on you; you act like a wild animal!

c) How's it going with your basketball?

d) I agree with you, that the teacher does seem to have it in for you.

e) You shouldn't act like that in school.

f) If I hear one more thing about you getting in trouble in school you will be sorry!

g) Other: _____

EARLY CHILD
COMMUNICATION STYLES (Cont.)

Your eleven year old says to you, "How come I have to take care of the yard and take the garbage out? Johnny's mother doesn't make him do all that stuff? You're not fair! Kids shouldn't have to do that much work. Nobody is made to do as much as I have to do."

Which of the following best describes how you would react?

a) Fine! I'll do it myself.
b) I don't care what other parents do; you have to do the yard work!
c) Look at it this way—your mother needs help around the house.
d) You're a spoiled brat!
e) How many other kids have you talked to about the work they have to do?
f) I used to think that to.

Other: _____

You have two daughters eight and six years old. Your oldest comes to you saying, "You are always yelling at me, you like Lisa better. You always take her side. I wish I could live with another family."

Which of the following best describes how you would react?

a) Start packing her clothes.
b) You children must learn to get along with one another.
c) That's an immature way to react.
d) Okay, little baby.
e) You really don't want to live with another family.
f) One more statement like that and I'll send you to another family.
g) Other:_____

NOTES:

EARLY CHILD
COMMUNICATION STYLES (Cont.)

Your five-year-old son becomes more and more frustrated when he can't get the attention of his mother and father and your two guests after dinner. The four of you are talking intently, renewing your friendship after a long separation. Suddenly you are shocked when your little boy loudly shouts, "You're all a bunch of dirty smelly old stinkbugs. I hate you!"

Which of the following best describes how you would react?

a) Laugh.
b) You must always respect your elders.
c) Look here, Mr. Fresh mouth.
d) Don't talk to our guests that way!
e) That's an immature way to handle your feelings.
f) If you have something you want to say, I suggest you say it nicely.
g) Other:_____

My Plan for Building Positive Relationships:

> **My specific concern:**
>
>
>
>
>
>
>

My usual responses:

Talking, lecturing, preaching

Punishing, shaming

Commanding

Other: _____

Criticizing, nagging

Threatening, warning

Becoming angry

I would like to change my behavior by doing more:

Listening

Encouraging

Practicing mutual respect

Communicating love

Acknowledging

Mirroring

Using door openers

Other:

> **I plan to make changes in the following situation(s):**
>
>
>
>
>
>
>
>

QUESTIONS PARENTS NEVER SEEM TO GET ANSWERS TO:

Can you hear me?

What are you, stupid?

But what's wrong with you?

How many times have I told you to stop that?

Why is this happening?

What did I do to deserve this?

Where did you get that idea?

Are you out of your mind?

When are you going to listen?

When are you going to learn?

What did I tell you?

What were you doing while you were out all this time?

How long have you been on that phone?

Don't you have homework?

Shouldn't you be doing your homework?

Where did I go wrong?

PARENT COMMUNICATION

One of the most valuable secrets to building positive relationships with your children is practicing the art of effective communication. In order to fine tune this skill, parents may find it helpful to **identify their own style of communicating** with their children and to **practice alternate methods of communication** where it seems warranted.

Remember: communication is the art of listening to feelings as well as being able to express them.

Suggestions:

1. Ask yourself what areas are of most concern to you in relation to your child.
2. How have you handled communication about these problems in the past?
3. What kind of person do you want your child to be?
4. What qualities do you value and admire in others that you would like to see in your child? (I.e., independence, responsibility, sensitivity to others, productivity, self-confidence...)
5. How might your child acquire these characteristics?

Beware of Static Communication Signals:

1. Messages sent are not the messages received. Nonverbal messages are sent even without verbal messages. It can be helpful to find out how your child perceives your verbal and nonverbal messages.
2. Mixing fact and opinion.
3. Sending double messages.
4. Forgetting that no two people see things exactly alike.

Avoid Some Typical Parent Responses:

Commanding, warning (threatening), preaching, advising, lecturing, giving solutions, probing, interrogating, judging, criticizing, disagreeing, blaming, interpreting, analyzing, or diagnosing, name-calling, shaming, consoling, distracting, humoring, withdrawing, and giving logical arguments.

TYPICAL PARENT RESPONSES

1. **Commanding**: Telling the child to do something, giving an *order* or *command*.
2. **Warning (threatening)**: Telling the child what the *consequences* will be if something occurs.
3. **Preaching**: Telling the child what *should* or *ought* to be done.
4. **Advising, suggesting, or giving solutions**: Telling the child how to *solve* a problem, giving advice or *suggestions*, or *providing answers*.
5. **Lecturing, teaching or giving logical arguments**: Trying to *influence* the child with facts, *counterarguments, logic,* or you own *opinions*.
6. **Judging, criticizing, disagreeing, and blaming**: Making *negative judgment* or *evaluation* of the child.
7. **Praising, agreeing**: Offering a *positive evaluation* or *judgment,* or *agreeing*.
8. **Name-calling, shaming**: Making the child *feel foolish*, putting higher into a *category, shaming*.
9. **Interpreting, analyzing, or diagnosing**: Telling the child what their *motives* are or *analyzing* why they are doing or saying something, communicating that you have *figured* them out.

10. **Sympathizing, consoling, reassuring, and supporting**: Trying to make the child *feel better,* talking them out of their feeling, trying to make their feeling go away, *denying* the strength of their feeling.

11. **Probing, questioning, and interrogating**: Trying to find *reasons, motives, and causes;* searching for more information to help *you solve the problem.*

12. **Distracting, humoring, and withdrawing**: Trying to get the child away from the problem; *withdrawing* from the problem yourself: *distracting* the child, *kidding* them out of it, *pushing* the problem *aside.*

EFFECTS OF TYPICAL PARENT RESPONSES

I feel the need to stop talking or to shut off.

I feel the need to be defensive.

I feel the need to argue, counterattack.

I feel inadequate or inferior.

I feel resentful or angry.

I feel guilty or bad.

I feel I'm being pressured to change – not accepted as I am.

I feel the other person doesn't trust me to solve my problem.

I feel I'm being treated as if I were a child.

I feel I'm not being understood.

I feel my feelings aren't justified.

I feel I've been interrupted.

I feel frustrated.

I feel I'm on the witness stand being cross-examined.

I feel the listener is just not interested.

Recognizing Barriers to Effective Communication

Using the following list of 'barriers,' read each item and write the reason why the parent's message may be ineffective in the space provided.

a) Blaming, judging

b) Providing solutions

c) Sarcasm

d) Venting anger

e) Name-calling
f) Threatening
g) Commanding
h) Preaching

Example: Ten year old left the Legos on the floor of the baby's room. **PARENT'S RESPONSE**: "That was so stupid. The baby could have choked." **BARRIER**: A. Blaming, judging

1. Kids fighting over which TV program to watch. **PARENT'S RESPONSE**: "Stop that fighting and turn off the TV right now!" **BARRIER**: _____

2. Daughter arrives home at 2:00 a.m. after agreeing to be home at midnight. Parent has been worried, but is relieved when she finally arrives. **PARENT'S RESPONSE**: "Well, I can see that you cannot be trusted. I am so angry with you. You're grounded for a month." **BARRIER**: _____

3. Twelve-year-old left gate to back yard open, endangering two years old. **PARENT'S RESPONSE**: "What did you want to do, kill the baby? I'm furious with you."

4. **BARRIER**: _____

5. Teacher sent a note home that an eleven-year-old boy was doing too much loud and 'filthy' talking in class. **PARENT'S RESPONSE**: "Come in here and explain why you want to embarrass your parents with your dirty mouth." **BARRIER**: _____

6. Child is dawdling and making parent late for an appointment. **PARENT'S RESPONSE**: "I would like for you to be more considerate." **BARRIER**: _____

7. Parent finds a mess after asking children to keep it clean for company. **PARENT'S RESPONSE**: "I hope you all had a lot of fun this afternoon at my expense." **BARRIER**: _____

8. Parent is repulsed by the sight and odor of child's dirty hands. **PARENT'S RESPONSE**: "Don't you ever wash your hands like other human beings? Get into the bathroom and wash." **BARRIER**: _____

9. Child is acting out to get your attention in front of guests. **PARENT'S RESPONSE**: "You little show off." **BARRIER**: _____

ALTERNATIVE CATEGORIES OF RESPONSE

Silence – Passive Listening:
Listening to a message without verbally responding. Communicates acceptance if the listener gives undivided attention to the speaker.

Simple Acknowledgment:
Verbal non-committal responses to a message.

Door Openers:
Verbal responses that are invitations to say more.

Mirroring:
Repeating messages in a way that conveys that you have heard the speaker.

Active Listening:
Messages that convey back empathetic understanding of a communication. Decoding and feeding back messages:

"Sounds like you feel _____, because _."

Communicate Your Feelings Using "I" Messages
Use I messages to communicate your positive feelings as well as to communicate things that bother you.

NOTES:

ATTENDING

Five basic skills in attending:

S – SQUARE: Face the child squarely.

O – OPEN: Adopt an open posture. In other words, do not cross your arms.

L – LEAN: Periodically lean toward the child.

E – EYE CONTACT: Maintain good eye contact; however, be aware that it is inappropriate in some cultures to look constantly into a person's eyes.

R – RELAX: Try to relax when you are practicing these skills of attending.

DOOR OPENERS

One of the most effective and constructive ways of responding to children's feeling-messages or problem-messages is to use "door openers." Door openers are responses that may invite the speaker to say more. These responses do not communicate the listener's judgments, ideas, or feelings, yet they open the door for the speaker to talk and share their ideas and feelings.

Simple Door Openers:

"I see."
"Oh."
"Mm hmmm."
"How about that."
"Interesting."
"Really."
"You don't say."
"No kidding."
"You did, huh."
"Is that so?"

More Explicit Door Openers:

"Tell me about it."
"Tell me more."
"Tell me the whole story."
"Let's discuss it."
"Shoot, I'm listening."
"I'd like to hear about it."
"I'd be interested in your point of view."
"Would you like to talk about it?"
"Let's hear what you have to say."
"Sounds like you've got something to say about this."
"This seems like something important to you."

Effects of Using Door Openers:

Door openers keep the listener's thoughts and feelings out of the communication process. As a result, the speaker may then feel encouraged to move in closer, open up, and pour out their feelings and ideas. Door openers also convey acceptance of the speaker and respect for higher as a person. They convey the following messages:

"You have a right to express how you feel."
"I might learn something from you."
"I really want to hear your point of view."
"I am interested in you.
"Your ideas are worthy of being listened to."
"I want to relate to you, get to know you better."
"I respect you as a person with ideas and feelings of your own."

THE TECHNIQUE OF ACTIVE LISTENING

When you use active listening:

✓ Listen for the feelings
✓ Be willing to take time
✓ Avoid "parroting"
✓ Respond in various ways
✓ Avoid putting your own message in the situation
✓ Respect your child's unwillingness to pursue a matter any further
✓ Have faith in your child

Active Listening Responses:

- That sounds to me like you are sad about…
- You feel upset about…
- You mean you are afraid of…
- I am not sure I understand. Do you mean you are disappointed that…
- You feel lonely right now because…
- Seems you are sure that…
- You hate that...
- You are irritated with me because…
- That's embarrassing for you to…
- It hurts when you…
- That makes you feel left out when…
- It is totally hopeless right now…
- Wow! That makes you feel proud about…

Don't Use Active Listening When...

- ✓ You have neither the time nor the desire to listen
- ✓ You are angry
- ✓ Your child wants specific information (when will you be home?)
- ✓ Your child does not want to talk about a problem
- ✓ You find it difficult to be separated from your child

COMMUNICATING YOUR FEELINGS
TO YOUR CHILDREN

Sending "I" Messages:

There are basically two ways parents can communicate their feeling to their children: they either send *You-messages* or *I-messages*. You messages can be put-downs of children. They may blame, criticize, ridicule, or judge. For example: "You're so rude. Must you constantly interrupt me?"

I-messages simply share how you feel about the consequences a child's behavior produces for you. When parents send I-messages, they take responsibility for their own feelings instead of blaming the child for their feelings. For example, the interrupted parent could respectfully say, "When I'm interrupted I feel discouraged because it seems my opinion is not important."

You-messages tend to reinforce misbehavior or produce ineffective results. I-messages are often unexpected and will frequently "defuse" the situation. Before expressing your feelings of displeasure to the child, consider that it is usually not the child's behavior per se which is displeasing you: but rather how it interferes with your needs or rights.

MODEL:

I-messages generally have three parts, though not necessarily in any particular order:

1. ***Describe the behavior*** that is interfering with you. Just describe, don't blame. Example: "When you don't come home on time..."

2. ***State you're feeling*** about the consequence the behavior produces for you.
Example: "...I worry that something might have happened to you..."

3. *State the consequence.*
   Example: "...because I don't know where you are."

Constructing an I-Message:

I Feel (state the feeling)
When (state the behavior)
Because (state the consequence)

Constructing an I-Message

Design an I-message for each situation below:

- Your son, who just got his driver's license is backing out of the driveway too fast.
- Your child forgets to feed the dog.
- You have just washed the car. Your child makes a design on it with muddy handprints.
- Your child comes to the table with dirty hands and face.
- Your child prevents you from having a conversation.

Consider a situation that you typically experience.

Whose problem is it?

If appropriate, construct an I-message for the situation.

> *Activity for the week: Practice using I-messages. Note the results.*

EXAMPLES OF "I" MESSAGES:

1. When you are cutting paper and making noise, I really feel annoyed because I am trying to sleep.
2. When you drive and exceed the speed limit, I feel frustrated and scared because it is not safe and may cause an accident.
3. When I am talking on the telephone and you turn up the volume on your stereo, I feel irritated because I cannot hear what is being said.
4. I feel very proud of you when you study for your algebra test because you earned a B+ on the test.

Feeling Words

WHEN NEEDS *ARE NOT* BEING MET	WHEN NEEDS *ARE* BEING MET
Hostile	**Exhilarated**
Animosity, Antagonistic, Appalled, Aversion, Cold, Contempt, Disgusted, Dislike, Distain, Hate, Horrified, Repulsed, Scorn, Surly, Vengeful, Vindictive	Ecstatic, Elated, Enthralled, Exuberant, Giddy, Silly, Slap-happy
Angry	**Excited**
Enraged, Furious, Incensed, Indignant, Irate, Livid, Mad, Outraged, Resentful, Ticked off	Alive, Amazed, Animated, Eager, Energetic, Enthusiastic, Invigorated, Lively, Passionate
Annoyed	**Inspired**
Aggravated, Bitter, Cranky, Cross, Dismayed, Disgruntled, Displeased, Exasperated, Frustrated, Grouchy, Impatient, Irked, Irritated, Miffed, Peeved, Resentful, Sullen, Uptight	Amazed, Astonished, Awed, Dazzled, Radiant, Rapturous, Surprised, Thrilled, Uplifted, Wonder
Upset	**Joyful**
Agitated, Alarmed, Discombobulated, Disconcerted, Disturbed, Disquieted, Perturbed, Rattled, Restless, Troubled, Turbulent, Turmoil, Uncomfortable, Uneasy, Unnerved, Unsettled	Amused, Buoyant, Delighted, Elated, Ecstatic, Glad, Gleeful, Happy, Jubilant, Merry, Mirthful, Overjoyed, Pleased, Radiant, Tickled
Tense	**Relaxed**
Antsy, Anxious, Bitter, Distressed, Distraught, Edgy, Fidgety, Frazzled, Irritable, Jittery, Nervous, Overwhelmed, Pressured, Restless, Stressed out, Uneasy	At ease, Carefree, Comfortable, Open
Afraid	**Curious**
Apprehensive, Concerned, Dread, Fearful, Foreboding, Frightened, Hesitant, Mistrustful, Panicked, Petrified, Scared, Suspicious, Terrified, Timid, Trepidation, Unnerved, Wary, Worried, Reserved, Sensitive, Shaky, Unsteady	Adventurous, Alert, Interested, Intrigued, Inquisitive, Fascinated, Spellbound, Stimulated
Vulnerable	**Confident**
Cautious, Fragile, Guarded , Helpless, Insecure, Helpless, Leery, Reluctant	Empowered, Proud, Safe, Secure, Self-assured
Confused	**Engaged**
Ambivalent, Baffled, Bewildered, Dazed, Flustered, Hesitant, Lost, Mystified, Perplexed, Puzzled, Skeptical, Torn	Absorbed, Alert, Ardent, Curious, Engrossed, Enchanted, Entranced , Involved
Embarrassed	**Hopeful**
Ashamed, Chagrined, Contrite, Guilty, Disgraced, Humiliated, Mortified, Remorse, Regretful, Self-conscious	Expectant, Encouraged, Optimistic
Longing	**Grateful**
Envious, Jealous, Nostalgic, Pining, Wistful, Yearning	Appreciative, Moved, Thankful, Touched
Tired	**Refreshed**
Beat, Burned out, Depleted, Exhausted, Fatigued, Lethargic, Listless, Sleepy, Weary, Worn out	Enlivened, Rejuvenated, Renewed, Rested, Restored, Revived, Energetic
Disconnected	**Affectionate**
Alienated, Aloof, Apathetic, Bored, Cold, Detached, Disengaged, Disinterested, Distant, Distracted, Indifferent, Lethargic, Listless, Lonely, Numb, Removed, Uninterested, Withdrawn	Closeness, Compassionate, Friendly, Loving, Openhearted, Sympathetic, Tender, Trusting, Warm
Sad	**Peaceful**
Blue, Depressed, Dejected, Despair, Despondent, Disappointed, Discouraged, Disheartened, Downcast, Downhearted, Forlorn, Gloomy, Grief, Heavy hearted, Hopeless, Melancholy, Sorrow, Unhappy	Blissful, Calm, Centered, Clear headed, Mellow, Quiet, Serene, Tranquil
Shocked	**Relieved**
Appalled, Disbelief, Dismay, Horrified, Mystified, Startled, Surprised	Complacent, Composed, Cool, Trusting
Pain	**Content**
Agony, Anguished, Bereaved, Devastated, Heartbroken, Hurt, Miserable, Wretched	Glad, Cheerful, Fulfilled, Satisfied

Feeling Words

Below is a list of feeling words. See if you can find other words to add to the list. Be careful with the use of the word *upset*. This is a "catch all" word that may not convey the depth of feeling.

Accepted	Safe
Afraid	Content
Angry	Accepting
Annoyed	Ignored
Appreciated	Good
Bad	Excited
Bored	Indifferent
Bothered	Scared
Brave	Stressed
Comfortable	Certain
Confused	Successful
Defeated determined	Undecided
Disappointed	OK
Discouraged	Encouraged
Disrespected	Respected
Down	Up
Embarrassed	Proud
Foolish	Confident
Guilty	Satisfied
Happy	Sad
Hurt	Loved
Interested	Turned off
Nervous	Relaxed
Pleased	Irritated
Proud	Ashamed
Surprised	Shocked
Trusted	Doubted
Rejected	

FINDING THE HIDDEN MESSAGE
LISTENING FOR FEELINGS

Directions: Behind the words, children often communication feelings. Read each statement and try to listen for the feelings being communicated. Discard the content and write the feeling or feelings you heard in the column at the right.

STATEMENT	FEELING
1. Dad, guess what? I saved the princess in the video game!	1.
2. Will you hold my hand when we go into nursery school?	2.
3. There's nothing to do around here.	3.
4. I'll never be as good as her. I keep trying and she is still better than me.	4.
5. I can't get all my homework done. My teacher gives too much work. What'll I do?	5.
6. All the kids went to the movies and I don't have anyone.	6.
7. He can go to school by himself and I'm older than he is.	7.
8. I shouldn't have been so mean to her.	8.

9. If I don't tie my shoes it's my business—they're my shoes.	9.
10. Am I doing this right? Is it good enough?	10.
11. I'd like to smack my teacher for making me stay after school. I wasn't the only one who was talking.	11.
12. You don't need to help me. I can do it myself.	12.
13. I'm too dumb to understand math. It's too hard.	13.
14. Leave me alone! You don't care what happens to me anyway. I don't want to talk to you!	14.
15. I don't want to play with him anymore. He's a dope.	15.
16. It's a good thing you guys are my parents.	16.
17. What should I do? I always seem to do the wrong thing.	17.

Points to Remember: Communication & Listening

-    Communication begins by listening and indicating you hear the child's feelings and meanings.
-    Effective listening involves establishing eye contact and posture that clearly indicate that you are listening.
-    Avoid typical parent responses: probing, criticizing, threatening, and lecturing...
-    Treat your children the way you would treat your best friend.
-    Mutual respect involves accepting the child's feelings.
-    Reflective listening involves hearing the child's feelings and meanings and stating this is so that child feels understood. It provides a mirror for the child to see himself or herself more clearly.
-    Learn to give open responses that accurately state what the other person feels and means.
-    Avoid closed responses that ignore the child's feelings, relaying that you have not heard or understood.
-    Let your child learn by resisting the impulse to impose your solutions.

MODULE 7

Developing Efective Communication and Listening Skills (Teens)

Dr. Joan D. Atwood

INTRODUCTION
(Teen Communication Styles)

One guaranteed aspect of the teenage life cycle is change. It seems as though they are going through a revolution—physical, emotional, mental and hormonal—and these changes can cause feelings of identity crisis, confusion and frustration. It is normal for teens to feel frustrated and sometimes become angry. The developmental task during this stage is for teens to develop a sense of self and to try to figure out where they fit in the world. In order to help your teen during this time of transition, communication is key.

HOW TO COMMUNICATE WITH YOUR TEEN

If there is talk about dating, driving, telephone use, curfew, drugs, sex, music, friends in your house, it is likely you are living with a teen. These are common topics in the teenage years. They are a lot easier to manage when parents and teens communicate effectively with each other.

Technically, **effective communication** occurs when the person sending the message makes it clear and easy to understand, and the person receiving the message understands the message as the sender intended. In the real world, especially in families, this is not always the case. Parents often are busy with work, household chores, and taking care of responsibilities to family and friends. Teens also are involved in many activities. The have academic and social demands of school, after school and weekend activities, and spending time with friends. With so much going on, it is no surprise that many do not take the steps needed to communicate clearly and to listen carefully. This often can lead to problems.

Why is communication so important during the teenage years?

As teens get older, they generally spend less time with parents and more time with their peers. They now need to make decisions on their own. They have to consider good vs. bad choices. At this time, they also are expected by others to take responsibility for their actions. Although teens are gaining more independence from their parents, they are not experienced in the ways of the world and need continuing parental guidance. Being sensitive to your teen's level of maturity when offering guidance helps in building greater self-confidence.

There are several techniques and behaviors that can increase good communication and reduce communication problems:

1. *Talk more often.*

The more you talk with each other, the more you have the chance to share important information. Good times to talk with your teen are before leaving for the office and school, during dinner, and on weekends. Try to plan at least one meal a day as a time when the family sits together and talks. Sometimes it does not matter what you talk about, just that you are talking to each other on a regular basis.

2. *Take extra time to share important messages.*

When you need to tell your teen something important, such as explaining the responsibilities of caring for a younger sister or brother, take the time to sit down with your teen and talk face to face. You also can write down the important details for your teen. Ask your teen to share with you what he understands your message to be. Your teen can use this same approach when she needs to share important messages with you.

When you communicate sensitively with your teen,
You are helping your teen grow up to be a responsible adult.

3. *As teens get older, parents need to understand that family rules must change.*

When Jack turned 16 and received his driver's license, he wanted to use the family car for weekend activities. He and his mother discussed rules for using the car and how car privileges would depend upon Jack's showing responsibility. His mom told him he needed to fill the car with gas before bringing it home, and he needed to have it home at the time he had promised. Setting up these rules in advance helped Jack know what was expected of him when he used the car. Knowing the rules also helped Jack to accept the consequences if he fell short of obeying the rules. His responsibilities were communicated to him and they were very clearly spelled out.

4. *Help your teen to figure out the kind of person she is becoming as she prepares for adult responsibilities.*

Mary and her parents watched a television show about teens and sex. After watching the show, Mary and her parents discussed their views about teen sexuality and responsibility. Mary needed to know her parents' views about teen sexual behavior but she also wanted to feel comfortable expressing her own ideas. Should she be faced with a difficult decision about her own sexual behavior, Mary would be more likely to make a good decision. She also is more likely to talk with her parents if there is an open line of communication.

5. ***Help your teen have better self-esteem.***

John compares himself often to other kids at school. He frequently feels like a failure, since he does not do as well on tests as others and is on the second string on the basketball team. John's father has listened to John complain about not being as good as other kids. He has expressed understanding of John's feelings. This usually helps John feel better. John's father also has been taking more time with John to do activities they both enjoy. John's father makes a special effort to make comments about things that John does well. In this way, John's father is helping John appreciate his own strengths and abilities.

6. ***Be a good role model for your teen in solving problems with other people.***

Jillian and her mother were out shopping one day when a salesperson was rude to them as they tried to return some clothes. Jillian's mother calmly told the salesperson that she expected to be permitted to return the items and asked if a manager were present who could assist with the return. The salesperson responded in a more helpful fashion. Jillian later asked her mother why she did not get angry at the salesperson. Her mother replied: "I was angry, but I have learned that I get better results when I stay calm and think about the best way to get the response I want to get from a person." In this way, Jillian had the opportunity to both observe and discuss a good way to handle problems with other people.

7. **Help your teen make important life decisions.**

Paul is trying to decide on a college. He wants to pick the best one, but he is not sure how to do this. His parents talk with him about his future goals, about the colleges that have programs that interest him, and also about colleges that the family can afford. They suggest that Paul call some of the colleges and arrange to visit the ones that are on the top of his list. They talk with Paul about other steps he can take to narrow his choices. His parents collaborate with Paul to figure out how to make good decisions, and they permit him to take the steps needed to make a good choice.

8. **Try to start each interaction with trying to understand your teen.**

Here's a simple secret that will help you in everything you do with your teen: No matter how hard it might be, try to start all interactions with your child with understanding, even if you do not fully agree or even quite comprehend what they are talking about.

Here's an example: Your teenage daughter is not doing her schoolwork, and instead is online with friends chatting. It drives you crazy because you're thinking, "If she fails another test, her average will go down and she will never get into college. What kind of future will she have?" Your teen, on the other hand is thinking, "I have to get online and talk with Matthew. If we do not make up after the fight we had in the hall today, all the other girls will be against me and I will have no one to hang out with at school tomorrow." Again, two different worlds.

Try to start by saying; "I understand how difficult it is for you when you have a fight with one of your friends. I also know that you need to pass this test tomorrow. Schoolwork is your job and it is your responsibility to do it to the best of your abilities. Let's sit down and think of a good way you can manage your time tonight." Be sure not to say "I understand, but..." which will simply disqualify what you've just said.

Start from a place of understanding, and try to put yourself in your child's shoes first before telling her what needs to change. I've found that doing this tends to "open kids' ears." Instead of feeling like they have to defend themselves against you, they actually listen.

9. Take the emotionality out of the equation.

Emotion is your enemy when you're trying to get through to your teen. Remind yourself that what she says and does is not a reflection on you. You may not like how she is behaving—or even how He is thinking—but keep your emotions out of it, even if his or her behavior impacts you. When you really think about it, there's no reason to be angry with your child for being him or herself. He may be making a poor choice, but the truth is, he might not yet have the skill set to make a better one. So your job is to help guide him to better choices so he can in turn develop a better skill set. When you realize what your job is as a parent, it will help you be less emotional. When you feel frustrated, remember, do not take it personally. Tell yourself that this is simply a problem to solve, And part of "parenting business as usual."

10. Ask curious questions...not loaded questions.

Ask your teen for his or her opinions and be collaborative. Let him see that you believe in him and that you're not mad at him for struggling in his life. When you let him see that you have faith in his abilities and he has the space to work things out on his own, you will begin to develop true confidence in him. Do not ask loaded questions that put your child on the defensive like, "Why can't you get up on time? What is wrong with you?" Instead, try opening a conversation with, "Eli, do you have any ideas for how you might get up on time?" If he says he does not know, offer a few of your own and ask which one would work for him. Let your teen know that his problems are *his* to solve. Do not step into his "box." Rather, you are there to help him figure out solutions—and to let him deal with the natural consequences of his behavior.

Your goal is to help your child think for him/herself, which will in turn help him/her feel like she has some control over his/her world. Listen openly to what she says and ask him/her to think critically about each choice. What will work and what will be problematic about each decision? What would be the natural consequences of each choice—and how would she feel about dealing with that?

11. Do not be needy; stand on your own two feet.

Do not "need" your teen's cooperation, validation, or good behavior. As soon as you need something from your child so that you can feel better, you have put yourself in a vulnerable position because she does not have to give it to you. When you need something and do not get it, you will naturally try harder by controlling and manipulating more. And your teen will become more and more defiant or passively compliant— neither of which is good.

The truth is, you do not need anyone else to build you up. You can validate yourself and solve your own problems. So if your child is acting out, that is his problem. *Your* problem is to decide how you will choose to behave toward him. That is in your hands, not his or hers. Ask yourself, "How do I want to behave, no matter how she is acting? What can I put up with and what can't I?" Take back your power and say to yourself, "If my child is screaming at me, instead of needing him to stop, I can turn around and walk away and not engage." Let him know you won't talk with him until he can approach you with civility. Here's the truth: when you aren't trying to get your child to change or shape up, you will be able to think of better choices for yourself. And your child will be less defiant because he will have no one to resist. When you're not trying to control him and you're not reacting to him, he will have to wrestle with himself rather than with you.

12. Do not do any talking until you're both calm.

Another technique is to avoid doing *anything* until you and your child have both calmed down. The fact is, you do not have to respond to your child when you are upset, or when your child is upset and in your face. You just do not. You can say nothing. You can take a few minutes or more if you need to. When emotions have evened out, you can sit down and talk with him/her. It is never good to try to bring up a difficult subject or resolve a conflict in the heat of the moment. So if either you or your child is upset, pause and come back when you can address things in a calmer way.

If you attempt a conversation with your child and he is rude or out of line, that is when you have to hold on to yourself and make sure you do not get dragged into a fight. If your relationship with your child is such that it is impossible to have an open, respectful conversation at this point in time, remember that it is still your job to stay firmly planted. Have a slogan that you say to yourself like, "I'm not going there no matter what." If you can do that consistently, over time the baiting and antagonism should calm down. The good news is that the more you refuse to engage, the easier it will get to stay calm.

13. *Do Something Together*

Spending time with your teen does not have to entail hours at the mall with his or her friends. Teach your teen how to make your famous cookies that she loves, or rent a movie you've both wanted to see on a weekday night. Just hanging out together at home or in a relaxed environment can help draw your teen out of her shell.

14. *Skip the Lecture*

Using accusatory words and lecturing your teen only causes higher to stop listening and shut down. Try to avoid using global phrases like, "You never" or "you won't" and instead focus on conveying to your teen how you feel about certain situations. Once you state your case, calmly listen to what your teen has to say and keep an open mind. If you've discovered something about your teen that needs to be addressed, try to control your anger and state how you feel in a blunt and matter-of-fact way.

Also, watch your body language. Crossing your arms or standing over your teen does not make for a very relaxing environment. He will clam up and all you'll likely hear from him is the slamming of his bedroom door.

15. *Keep it Simple*

You do not need to have a deep, philosophical conversation with your teen to connect. If simply asking how his/her day was only elicits a shrug and one-worded answer, try asking a more specific question, like what she did in science class that day or how his/her basketball team is preparing for their upcoming tournament. Having simple, daily conversations will help give your insight into your teen's world and will help higher to open up about how his/her everyday life is going.

16. *Give Her Breathing Room*

You do not need to smother your teen with questions to make it seem like you are interested in his/her life. Most teens value their space, and giving it to him/her shows that you trust him/her. If your teen knows that you trust him/her, she will be more likely to come to you to talk.

17. *Have Family Meals*

There are few things a teenager loves more than food, right? Eating dinner together as often as possible (try for at least three times a week) is a great way to get caught up on each other's lives. Ask your teen to turn his/her phone off or leave it in his/her room so she is not distracted by incoming texts and social media. You will be amazed what you can learn while sharing a meal together.

18. *Chat While Working Together*

Forced eye contact and face-to-face conversations can make anyone, especially teens, uneasy. Chat with your teen while you are both working on something or doing household chores like shoveling snow or raking leaves. You might find your teen becomes more talkative if she is keeping his hands busy or doing something else productive.

19. *Connect Online*

No, it is not the same as having a real conversation, but times are changing so you might as well go with the flow. While you should not ditch face-to-face conversation completely, you might find your teen is more open when you wade into his/her digital world. Start off with a silly, one-sentence email. If your teen bites and engages in the back-and-forth banter, you can sneak in a question or two about her day that might get you an actual response.

Nervous around technology? Even better. Ask your teen to show you how to email or text.

20. *Create a Ritual*

Perhaps you can get a pedicure together. Or indulge in your shared sweet tooth at your favorite cupcake shop. Play a pickup game of basketball. Whatever you do, try to have a monthly ritual that you and your teen always do together. Making it the same time every month (for example, on the 15th, or the third Thursday) will make your teen feel special and give him her something to look forward to. She might not admit it, but your teen likes to have your one-on-one attention, so make it a point to schedule regular "dates."

21. *Talk about Your Youth*

Reminiscing about when you were young will help your teen see you more as a person and less like a parent. While talking about anything illegal or dangerous is not smart, letting your teen in on a few of your past adventures and debacles might make him/her more likely to tell you about some of his/hers. If she makes you privy to this information, remember — listen, keep an open mind, and do not lecture!

NOTES:

LISTENING

A lot of good parent-teen communication involves listening.

The most important thing parents can do to improve communication with their teens is to listen to them. Listening to their teens helps parents to have more influence in their teens' lives. They feel that their parents understand them. And they feel that they matter and that they can depend on their parents to support and protect them. By listening to teens, parents get across messages of caring and safety.

Listening helps parents stay in touch with their teens' experiences and feelings even though their teens are spending more and more time away from them. Ultimately, listening begets listening. Most parents would like their teens to listen to them more. By parents listening to their teens, teens are more likely to listen, on their own, to their parents. The next time you sit down with your teen, ask her to tell you about something about his or her life and quietly hear what she has to say.

Do not be afraid to talk about the tough topics.

Involvement in problem behaviors such as sex and drug use can be part of experimentation during the teen years. Even good kids experiment. Parents are sometimes uncomfortable with these types of discussions and sometimes shy away or to give responses that say to your child, "This is something we do not talk about." The problem with avoiding these tough topics is that parents risk not knowing when their children may be getting into trouble. A parent may not realize that a teen's experimenting has gone too far and he has gotten in over his head.

Take teens and sex, for example. Teens are going to have many questions about sex, and they are going to have sexual feelings and thoughts. When teens have questions about their thoughts or feelings, parents who give them support and understanding are more likely to have teens who do not act impulsively when faced with a decision about sex. These teens are more informed about what they are feeling and thinking and about the consequences of acting on their thoughts and feelings. When teens understand what may happen if they engage in sexual activity and that their parents are not afraid to talk with them and to help them find answers about sex, these teens are better protected from the pressures of others to engage in sexual behaviors.

You can do several things to make dealing with tough topics easier:

- Check in with your children regularly, know where your children are, and check out concerns you have about your children's behavior. This will make it more likely that you will learn about trouble in the early stages and will have a better chance of helping your teen before things get out of hand.

- Encourage your child to invite friends to your house for the afternoon or for dinner. You can learn a lot about your teen's life by making your home a comfortable place for friends.
- Talk with other parents who you respect about their parenting styles.

POSSIBLE PROBLEMS

What to do about disagreements that will not go away.

Sometimes it is the day-to-day disagreements between parents and teens that can leave parents feeling powerless and wishing they knew what to do. Parents and teens often find themselves bickering about household responsibilities, curfews, friends, and activities. A lot of this bickering occurs because teens and parents view these day-to-day problems in very different ways. Take for example a teen's responsibility of caring for his room. For many teens, the neatness of their bedrooms is not a main concern. Friends and activities outside the home are often their central priorities. For many parents, their teens' lack of care for their bedrooms may make them feel like the teens do not respect the parents' values. The good news is many sloppy teens respect their parents and grow up to be responsible adults. But until they become responsible for their own homes, they may not feel that keeping their room clean is very important.

Many parents of teens find themselves constantly pleading with their teens to clean their rooms, or they clean the teen's room themselves, or they just accept a teen's messy room.

Brian and his mother have been battling over this issue for several months. Brian's mother is feeling frustrated because Brian's room is always a mess. Brian's view is that his room is his private space that he can maintain as he pleases. If he does not mind the mess, why should his mother? When Brian's mom yells at him for his lack of responsibility and grounds him for the weekend, nothing has been done to successfully solve the problem. Brian and his mother become more convinced that this problem is a "battle of the wills" rather than something that can be solved together. What is another way of handling this?

Mom and Brian can make more progress if they are willing to have some give and take about Brian's room, since teens do need space that is their own. Mom and Brian could discuss the main things that need to be cleaned or organized in Brian's room, such as no food in the room, or dirty clothes that are to be put in a hamper or basket. Brian and his mother can discuss the types of rewards that will be gained or lost depending upon his keeping his part of the bargain. Reaching an agreement that both mom and Brian like may take a little time. Putting their agreement in writing is a good way to increase the likelihood of Brian's cooperation. Brian's mother also must follow through by giving or taking away privileges according to the agreement. For Brian to hold up his end of the agreement, his mother must hold up hers.

What to do when talking is going nowhere.

Talking is not always easy between parents and teens. Sometimes no matter how hard they try to communicate with their teens, it seems as though nothing is getting. When this happens, it is necessary to reconsider "HOW" you are communicating with your teen.

COMMUNICATION CLOSERS AND OPENERS

Things that close the door to good communication with your teen include:

- Talking down to your teen
- Being judgmental and critical of your teen
- Refusing to listen to your teen's point of view

Things that open the door to good communication with your teen include:

- Make it clear that you are ready and willing to listen to your teen. "I really care about what you think." "Your ideas are important to me." "Tell me how you see it."
- Find activities that you enjoy doing together. Sometimes teens find it difficult to share what is on their minds during face-to-face conversation. Doing an activity together, such as playing games on the computer, preparing a meal together, working on a hobby, or traveling around town can make conversation flow more easily. Teens will say more when they feel relaxed.
- Permit your teen some privacy. Teens need time to themselves and the right not to share everything with their parents. They will be more willing to share the important things with you if they feel respected by you. Permitting independence from you is a great way to show a teen respect.
- Allow your teen to have opinions that differ from yours. The freedom for teens to have their Own ideas and views helps teens to become emotionally mature as they move toward adulthood and need to think on their own.

	What to do	Why it matters
Be Clear and Calm	If your teen breaks rules, be calm in Dealing with him or her. It is okay to take a break and relax before you talk with your child. Once you feel calm, sit down with your child and let him or her know why you are disappointed in his or her actions, The consequences for his or her actions, and the actions you would like him or her to take in the future.	Your teen needs for you to have rules for his behavior, but he needs to understand the rules and the rules should be appropriate for his age. When you remain calm, you help your teen to be calm, and you get your message across the way you intend.

	What to Do	Why it Matters
Support	If you teen says she needs you, make yourself Available to be there. Remind your teen that you are in his/her corner and available to help He/she deal with problems and decisions. Let your teen know that you do not do not expect her to be perfect. When she makes mistakes, help her to learn important lessons from them and to think about ways to not make the same mistakes again.	No matter how old they are, teens need their parents' support. Although they may think they are ready to take on the world, they know they are not ready to do it without their parents' Help. Being there to help them when they need it, allowing them to make mistakes along the way, is helping your teen to gain the strength she needs to be independent from you When the time comes.

	What to Do	Why it Matters
Seek Solutions	Tell your teen you want to work through the problem with him/her. Let him/her know that you believe there is a way to solve it. Talk Together about what each of you think might make things better. Try out some of your ideas. If you find that you and your teen are not able to find a solution that works, find other people who can help. Family members, friends, or professionals can assist you and you're teen to work through difficult problems.	There are solutions to problems no matter how difficult. You will be better able to help your teen work through problems if you believe there are ways to resolve them. Communicating this belief helps teens to feel better about their abilities to make positive changes in their lives.

MODULE 8

Emotions and Avoiding Daily Battles

WHAT WOULD YOU DO?

Directions:

Choose the response that is closest to what you might do in each given situation. Talk it over among your group and decide upon a choice you can all agree on. If none of the choices are your preferred response, fill in the choice for **"other"** and try to suggest an alternate response.

1. Your teen has come home and announced that she was sent down to the principal's office for talking too much in class. She states that she *"hates that **old** @? ***$"* and her *"lousy teacher"*. You respond by:

    a. Getting an aspirin.
    b. Saying "You what? You were sent to the principal's office!"
    c. Saying "Well that should teach you."
    d. Saying "Now then, your teacher isn't that bad is he?"
    e. Saying "Sweetheart, you have to learn some self-control."
    f. Saying "You'd better learn to adjust to all kinds of teachers."
    g. Other_____

2. Your 15-year old announces the following at dinner: "School doesn't mean anything. All you do is learn a lot of garbage that doesn't do you any good. There's a lot of other ways to get ahead in this world and I don't need no college!" Your response is to:

- Say "You feel that way because you're not doing well in school."
- Say "You're not thinking clearly."
- Say "College can be *the* most wonderful experience you'll ever have."
- Say "What will you do if you don't go to college?"
- Tell him/her to wait a couple of years before deciding to go to college.
- Correct his/her grammar.
- Other_____

3. Your 13 year old complains to you about a young sister. *"Will you please keep her away from my stuff? She keeps taking my things!"* Your response is to say:

- "She's only a kid. There's no reason to get crazy!"
- "Why don't you just put your things away?"
- "If you'd stop teasing her she wouldn't bother you!"
- "Stop complaining!"
- "You're acting like a baby yourself"
- "OK, I'll tell her."
- Other_____

WHAT WOULD YOU DO?

4. Your 16 year old insists on going to a party until 2 a.m. The crowd that will be there has a horrible reputation, but your teen claims, "everyone else is allowed to go". Your reaction is to:

   - Tell him to ask his mother (father).
   - Explain that he has poor taste in friends.
   - Warn that he had better not go if he knows what's good for him.
   - Tell him to make new friends.
   - Lock him in his room.
   - Argue that not everyone is going to the party.
   - Other_____

5. Your 14-year-old son sadly states that he can't make friends at school. He claims that the other students are all in their own groups. "Most of them won't even talk to me," he states. You respond by saying:

   - "It can't be all that bad."
   - "All kids go through this sometime."
   - "You're just feeling sorry for yourself."
   - "That's not true. You have plenty of opportunities to make friends."
   - "What are you doing wrong?"
   - "Why don't you try advertising?"
   - Other_____

6. Your 12 year old comes home complaining and swearing. Her comments are vulgar and insulting. You react by:

   - Swearing back.
   - Warning that one more statement like that and you'll "wash her mouth out with soap".

- Saying, "Where did you get the idea that you could talk to me like that? When I was your age I would never have spoken like that to one of my parents."
- Saying, "You have a filthy mouth!"
- Telling her that she is only saying that to get at you.
- Putting a towel over your eyes and saying, "Help me Lord!"
- Other_____

DEALING WITH NEGATIVE EMOTIONS:

✓ Construct plans for dealing with situations that evoke negative emotions.
   o The expression of negative emotions is in large part determined by gender and/or culture.
   o Unfortunately, the United States has a limited repertoire for language and/or dealing these emotions.
   o Feeling persecuted, vengeful, rejected, disappointed, blaming or condemning others, and attitudes of self-righteousness may affect the way in which individuals deal with anger.

✓ Learn to express anger appropriately and or use reasoning, logical consequences, and cooperative strategies for parenting.
   o Inappropriate expression of anger can be damaging in children's experience.
   o Seize opportunities to clearly demonstrate positive emotions to children where possible.
   o Emotions of parents and children flow in reciprocal, escalating cycles (i.e., positive emotions elicit cooperation and positive emotional responses, while negative emotions elicit resistance and negative emotional responses and so on).

✓ Express anger in a way that informs children that their actions are inappropriate or unacceptable.
   o Emotions are linked with reactions (and therefore parenting skills).
     ▪ Weak emotional responses from parents may not convey clear messages.
     ▪ Strong emotional responses can be problematic when parents' reactions are incompatible with more appropriate reactions for child rearing.
       For example: Angry parents may avoid, criticize, or punish children at moments when children instead need support, instruction, or clarification.

✓ Utilize communication and listening skills.
   o Be assertive, but avoid using "I-messages" as angry "you-messages" said in a different way.
   o When parents send hostile messages, it is very difficult for children to interpret them as non-threatening.

✓ It is helpful to remember that emotions are transient.
   o Emotions can only be maintained by an individual for a time.

Other suggestions:

Stress-inoculation, self-instructional training, relaxation-desensitization, cathartic expression, assertiveness training, developing problem solving skills, and exploring the meaning of stimuli which elicit anger.

DEALING WITH YOUR OWN EMOTIONS

Emotions can be created from a thought or belief. For example, we may believe that life should or must be a certain way: then we become upset (sometimes overly upset) when life doesn't meet with our expectations. If you hold some of the following beliefs, you may see negative events as catastrophes rather than simple annoyances, and you may blame yourself, others, or life for negative situations. You may even believe that you cannot handle a situation, even though a more useful belief would be that you can handle it (even if you don't like it).

I should be perfect.
I should be right
I should be the best
I should make a good impression.
I should win.
People should give me my own way.
I should succeed.
People should recognize my contribution.
I should always be in control.
Life should be fair.
I should please everyone.
Life should be easy.

A key to changing these negative patterns of thinking is to decide that there is no reason why things should be as we want them. If we recognize this belief, we may become annoyed or disappointed, but we won't experience these situations as catastrophes.

If you find yourself strongly upset, see if you can find a "**SHOULD**" belief that is contributing to your distress. If so, to change your feelings you may want to try following these steps:

✓ Decide to look at the situation as unfortunate, not as catastrophic.
✓ Decide to accept imperfections, not to blame.

✓ Decide you can take what life dishes out.
✓ Decide there's no rational reason why any person or situation should follow your orders.

DEALING WITH ANGER

This Module provides some experiential exercises and suggestions regarding anger. In Module 9 and Module 10, anger is discussed in much more detail.

What do I get angry about?

✓ The illusion of helplessness and being out of control.
✓ The illusion that children's misbehavior reflects badly on us.
✓ The painful acknowledgment that children can enrage us.
✓ Re-experiencing the hurt of old wounds.
✓ Not getting our needs met.
✓ Unfulfilled expectations

What can be done?

✓ Exit the scene and make amends later. Inform children that the anger is not permanent.
✓ Don't make decisions when angry or highly agitated.
✓ Take a time-out for yourself, cool down, and then make decisions from a more rational place.
✓ Remember the goal is to change behavior, not to hurt.

Talk about your feelings. Tell people when things bother you.

Use "I" messages rather than attack.
Use brief messages in an authoritative, nonjudgmental, tone of voice.

Vent anger in appropriate ways.
Find a physical way to release your energy, like hitting a pillow, running or doing push-ups.

Sit on your hands, count to 10, and breathe deeply.

Make your own "self-talk tape." Use anger as the signal to press "PLAY".

Keep "self-focused" rather than "other focused." Assertion rather than aggression or passivity.)

Try changing the situations that make you angry.

Formulate plans for dealing with anger in the future. In detail, visualize the success of the plans.

When children express their anger, try to be empathic.

Use active listening, mirroring; suggest time-out to cool down or other appropriate methods for venting and controlling anger.

---

*Remember: **How you deal with your anger
provides a model for your children as well.***

NOTES:

JUST FOR YOU

Relieving Your Stress:

Being a parent is a twenty-four-hour-a-day, seven-day-a-week job. It's no wonder, then, if we find ourselves under stress some of the time! Stress is a physical and emotional response to events we find upsetting. There are several ways to ease and handle stress that you may wish to use in the coming weeks:

- ✓ Use deep breathing for about fifteen seconds. Let your breathing pace itself—don't force it. Practice silently saying "calm" as you breathe in and "down" as you breathe out until you begin to feel relaxed.
- ✓ Use positive self-talk. Say simple, upbeat statements: "Be calm." "Take it easy." "You're okay."
- ✓ Prepare yourself for a situation you think might be stressful. Take a few deep breaths and talk to yourself before facing the situation.
- ✓ Think of a situation as an opportunity or a challenge, rather than as something stressful or something you can't handle.

✓ Every day, accept yourself and take time to concentrate on your positive qualities. Make self-affirming statements: "I'm capable." "I'm worthwhile." "I make my own decisions."

✓ Take a few moments now to jot down some affirming statements about your positive beliefs and behaviors.

> **Begin practicing stress reduction this week.**

WHAT INDIVIDUALS GET ANGRY ABOUT AND WHY

✓ Beliefs about others and ourselves can affect our emotional state.

✓ Parent's emotions are typically effected by their wants and needs.

✓ Emotions are largely automatic
Thus, parents might consider the idea that some of their reactions to children's behavior may be related to an unconscious search for "wholeness" and/or re-experiencing situations that stimulate the hurt of their own "wounds" from childhood.

✓ Anger can be considered a reaction to experiencing other emotions.
For example, feelings of hurt, disappointment, frustration, helplessness, and loss of control, have been known to trigger angry responses.

✓ Individuals may experience anger if they believe that they:
  o Lack parenting skills
  o Are incompetent, or
  o Are unable to cope with or control events

✓ Individuals may use anger as a way to control others.

✓ Anger may represent a lack of self-focus and emotional responsibility.

✓ Anger may be an evolutionary protective mechanism.
Thus, while anger may prepare persons to perceive and remove obstructions, it may also interfere with empathic concern for children.

✓ Anger may arise in conjunction with situational pressures.
(I.e., work, difficulties in relationships with spouses, stress) – All of which contribute to parents' negative attributions about their functioning as parents.

AVOIDING DAILY BATTLES

✓ Decrease reactivity, commands, criticism and lectures, which invite defiance.

✓ Increase cooperative statements (i.e., "When…", "As soon as…")

✓ Increase effective communication
   o Listen empathically and acknowledging feelings.
   o Talk less – i.e., using one-word reminders).
   o Decrease use of "You" statements and begin using "I" messages.

✓ Allow children to learn from logical consequences.

✓ Allow opportunities for children to become problem solvers.
   o Provide choices within limits.
   o Provide time for family consultations and meetings for agreements.

✓ Learning to Let Go
   o Give children opportunities to make decisions.
   o Decrease controls to increase autonomy in appropriate situations.
   o Allow children a voice in choosing clothing, food, how to spend free time, when to do class work, etc.

✓ Be supportive and encouraging, even if children don't succeed.

HANDLING CONFLICT IN ADULT RELATIONSHIPS

Exploring alternatives can be used to address problems with children. It can also be used when a conflict occurs with a spouse, a friend, or a relative. You can use the steps for exploring alternatives to negotiate agreements.

- ✓ Understand the problem.
- ✓ Use brainstorming to find possible solutions (alternatives).
- ✓ Consider the suggested solutions.
- ✓ Choose a solution.
- ✓ Make or obtain a commitment to a solution and set a time to evaluate.

Rudolph Dreikurs, a psychiatrist and author, identified four important principles for handling conflict:

- ✓ Maintain mutual respect. Avoid fighting or giving in. Use reflective listening and "I" messages.
- ✓ Identify the real issue. You may be discussing money or sharing responsibilities. But what's being discussed is seldom the real issue. Many times the real issue is who is right, who will be in charge, or fairness. You can say something like, "It seems to me we're both interested in being right. I wonder how this will help us solve the problem."
- ✓ Change the agreement. In a conflict, the persons involved have made an agreement to quarrel. You can change the agreement by changing your own behavior. Be willing to compromise if necessary.
- ✓ Invite participation in decision-making. An agreement comes when both persons suggest solutions and settle on one both are willing to accept. If this doesn't happen, all you can do is state your intentions: 'since we aren't willing to find a solution acceptable to both of us, I choose "Your intentions simply tell what you will do—not what the other person does.

If you have a conflict in your adult relationships you'd like to resolve, decide how to use the steps for exploring alternatives and the principles of conflict resolution to handle the conflict. How will you begin the discussion?

A WORD ABOUT RELATIVES AND FRIENDS

Sometimes others don't understand your child-rearing methods and may interfere with them. You can recognize their feelings and state your reasons for your actions. ("I understand you're uncomfortable with the way I'm raising _____, but I find this works for me.") You may have to confront others and give them choices ("I don't agree with treating _____ that way. It's discouraging. If you choose to continue, we'll stop visiting for a while until you and I can come to an agreement."). This may be hard for you to do, but you have to decide what's best for your child.

WHOSE PROBLEM IS IT?

The Concept of Problem Ownership:

Effective responses to parent-child concerns depend upon who owns the problem. For example, if the parent owns the problem it is helpful for the parent to incorporate the use of "I-messages": if the child owns the problem, it is helpful for parents to mobilize listening skills. You can determine who owns the problem by asking yourself these questions when something happens:

1. Who does this problem really affect?
2. Who is having a problem with whom?
3. Whose responsibility is it to take care of this problem?

Examples:

- A parent is trying to watch a favorite TV show and the children are in the same room laughing and teasing each other. The parent has the problem: how to stop the behavior so the parent can watch the show. The children are not concerned with the interruption. They may simply want attention. The fact that the parent is busy is the parent's problem. The parent has to handle the situation.
- A child is having difficulties with a friend. The child's problem in no way affects the parent or interferes with the parent's rights as a person. It's up to the child to handle the problem (unless there is a danger to the child or someone else).

Summary:

In every parent-child relationship three situations may occur:

1. The child owns the problem because there is some obstacle that prevents him/her satisfying a need.
2. There is no problem since the child is satisfying his/her own needs without interfering with a parent satisfying their needs.
3. The parent owns the problem because the child is satisfying his/her needs, but his/her behavior is interfering with the parent's satisfying a need of their own.

PROBLEM LIST

Directions:

In the space provided, mark a "P" if the parent owns the problem and a "C" if the child owns it.

> Child misbehaves in public.
> Fighting with brothers and sisters.
> Leaving belongings around the house.
> Misbehavior at school
> Homework is not done
> Not going to bed on time
> Uncooperative during the morning routine
> Messing up the kitchen
> Misbehavior at the dinner table
> Not getting along with peers
> Coming home late
> Writing on walls
> Borrowing the car without permission
> Hanging out with the 'wrong' crowd
> Child unhappy about assigned chores

POINTS TO REMEMBER

- ✓ Emotions serve a purpose. They provide the energy for us to act.
- ✓ Take responsibility for your own emotions and encourage your teen to do the same.

Typical negative emotions of teenagers include:

> Anger
> Apathy
> Boredom
> Sadness and depression

Guilt

Fear and anxiety

Stress

✓ You can help your teen handle negative emotions through listening, encouragement, and involving the teen in constructive family responsibilities.

✓ To redirect our teens' misbehavior we must change not only how we respond, but also what we feel as well.

✓ We create our own emotions by holding certain beliefs about things that happen in our lives.

✓ We catastrophize by translating our preferences into needs.

✓ When we make demands on life, we are involved in irrational thinking.

▪ Some typical irrational beliefs of parents regarding teens are:

   ✓ To be a good parent I must (**should**) have the approval of everyone in the community.

   ✓ I should (**must**) be competent in all aspects of parenting.

   ✓ Things should turn out the way I want them to.

   ✓ People are victims of circumstances and should not try to change what can't be changed.

   ✓ I should take the responsibility for my teenager's behavior. If I were a more effective parent, my teen would always be well behaved.

✓ Your responses to your teen's misbehavior are created by what you tell yourself about the misbehavior. You can change your responses by changing your thinking (your belief).

▪ Irrational responses can be changed by using the following strategies:

   ✓ Admit your feelings, accept yourself, and make a commitment to change.

   ✓ Identify the purpose of your negative emotions.

   ✓ Watch your tone of voice.

   ✓ Watch your nonverbal behavior.

- ✓ Distract yourself.
- ✓ Avoid your first impulse and do the unexpected.
- ✓ Learn to relax.
- ✓ Use your sense of humor.
- ✓ Work directly on changing your irrational beliefs.

NOTES:

Dr. Joan D. Atwood

LET ME BE A CHILD

Let me dream. Share my joy when my dreams come true.
Share my tears when they don't.
Let me feel secure in my home.
Help me realize that love is always there.
That I can depend on you no matter what.
Let me run. Let me laugh. Let me play.
And most of all, let me be a child.

Anonymous

MODULE 9

All about Anger

THE BRAIN OF AN ANGRY TEEN

The Brain of an Angry Teen

First and foremost, it is important to realize that even though adolescents might engage in adult-like behaviors or try to act like adults, they do not have the brains of adults. The brains of adolescents are still developing, and they continue to do so into their early to mid-twenties. That considered, it does not make sense to really expect children to act like we do as adults. In fact, kids often perceive things in a very different way than we do, in part due to faulty or distorted thinking. The danger comes in when they use this distorted thinking to justify or rationalize their angry behavior.

What makes some teenagers display angry and aggressive behavior, while others are calm and in control? A growing number of scientists are looking at the same area of the brain that is involved in A.D.D. and A.D.H.D., the delicate limbic system. Research demonstrates alterations of function in the limbic system causes changes in emotional responses as rage, fear, reasoning, and impulse control. The limbic system located deep in the brain's interior is associated with the roots of anxiety, panic, and fear. The limbic system stays in overdrive due to an excessive production of sex hormones. The teen years are a time of continuous changes in brain chemistry.

According to Frank Goodwin, a psychiatry professor at Brian Washington University, the environment activates a genetic vulnerability. Too much stress and too little support can lead to increased depression. However, the majority of evidence points to disturbed brain function and the overproduction of certain chemical and under production of others. Studies done at the University of Illinois Medical School found children and teens with aggressive and disruptive behavior all had low levels of the major inhibitory neurotransmitter serotonin. Serotonin levels are the most accurate predictors of how teens and children will react to punishment? Serotonin transmits electrical impulses in the brain from one neuron to another. Smooth transmission of impulses is interrupted when serotonin levels are low. When this occurs the brain receives mixed signals. According to Ronald Kotulak, author of *Inside the Brain,* scientists now believe that along with the nations increase in violence, low serotonin may be responsible for a steady increase in depression, especially among children.

During adolescence, the teen brain undergoes a multitude of changes, the neural pathways, the connections between neurons affecting emotional skills; physical ability and mental cognition are not yet developed. The teen brain has a tremendous capacity for emotional growth. Girls usually develop much faster than boys. If a child uses drugs, emotional growth is delayed, and the ability to sort out, reason, and resolve is never fully developed. Kids turn to drugs as a cosmetic quick fix when parents are not *'there"* for emotional support during the teen years.

Amino acid blood tests done on one hundred teens and children at the Pain & Stress Center all reflected a major deficiency of neurotransmitters. When the deficiencies were corrected with amino acid supplementation, behavior problems ranging from aggression, anger, A.D.D., A.D.H.D., behavioral disorders, poor concentration, and depression, all diminished remarkably. Inborn metabolic errors, chronic stress/anxiety as well as an over consumption of junk food, caffeine, sugar, and alcohol cause neurotransmitter deficiencies. Chronic stress burnout can also kill vital brain cells.

Some scientists report children can inherit a tendency toward anger and aggression through aggressive genes. This predisposes a teen to anger, violence, and depression; and it is very likely that the child could pass the gene on to his children. Children are the genetic and environmental products of their parents. The cause of negative behavior can be a direct result of not only genes, but also brain chemistry. The delicate balance between the limbic system, amygdala, and prefrontal cortex is the key to where critical judgments are formed. In the case of most teens the limbic system is in overdrive, the amygdala is a storehouse of unresolved anxiety and the prefrontal cortex is sleepwalking. The genes that direct your child's behavior are chemicals that direct a combination of more chemicals. The brain has its own pharmacy, the only drugs you will ever need are already there.

Children who have an alcoholic parent can inherit the alcoholic gene, and demonstrate the same amino acid deficiencies that cause the craving for alcohol. GABA and glutamine, two major neurotransmitters shut off the craving switch in the brain. When the brain chemistry is in balance, impulsive and aggressive behavior patterns do not dominate brain function.

Serotonin is a major inhibitory neurotransmitter, a chemical that transmits electrical impulses in the brain from one neuron to another. If there is a defect in the serotonin processing in the brain, impulsive or violent behavior can result. Serotonin can enable impulses in the brain to harmonize. Serotonin-producing cells send out over five hundred thousand connections to cells in every part of the brain. Serotonin is the only neurotransmitter that is able to do that. The prefrontal cortex is an organizational part of the brain. If there is an injury in that area one of the outcome can be impulsive, uncontrollable, and violent behavior.

There is no simple solution to teen anger and violence. In addition to amino acids, parents should consider therapy sessions with a qualified therapist. Therapists are trained in talk therapy. Therapists can help troubled teens sort out their feelings so they feel better about themselves, and most importantly, resolve anxiety. The longer negative feelings stay buried, the more powerful they become. This brain activity not only uses all available neurotransmitters, it sets up a chain reaction that causes them to withdraw and allow their problems to go unresolved.

Parents who put their children on Prozac, Zoloft, Serzone, or any other prescription drug to elevate the serotonin level are only using available neurotransmitters. Drugs do not create new needed neurotransmitters. Drugs only mask symptoms and repress anger that should be resolved. There are neurotransmitter formulas available that can be given to children and teens safely without the possibility of addiction or long-term side effects.

The key is to correct neurotransmitter imbalances in the brain and control aggression by adjusting brain levels of serotonin. Available serotonin declines in situations when chronic stress/anxiety is in control of a person's life. Impulsive and angry behaviors become a way of life setting the stage for possible violent behavior.

An amino acid blood test can be done to establish exact amounts of amino acid deficiencies. The blood that flows through the brain is a virtual map to its activities.

Warning Signs of a Teen Anger Problem

Keep an eye on your teens for signs of an anger problem. If anger problems are not addressed in a timely manner, it can lead to incidents of teen violence. Here are some signs that an anger problem exists:

- Regular loss of temper over small things
- Property damage during times of anger
- Victim of a bully or prolonged teasing
- Drug and alcohol use
- Regular arguments with family and friends (may begin to turn physical)
- Cruelty to animals

What you can do to help manage teen anger

As a parent, you can help your teen work through his or her anger issues, preferably before they become serious enough to result in teen violence. Most teen anger problems stem from frustrations, fears and rejection. Here are some things you can do to help:

- Offer your support and love
- Listen carefully and engage in conversation. Try to understand the underlying issue beyond the surface behavior
- Be on the lookout for anger triggers and try to find ways to deflect it
- Teach your teen that anger is understandable, but that it needs to be controlled
- Show your teenager how you find positive outlets for your anger and frustration
- Help your teen recognize anger-related feelings and practice control

Suggestions You Can Give Your Teen to Deal with Anger

You can help you teen learn anger management techniques by sharing the following with him or her:

- Deep breathing can help calm and relax your teen
- Suggest that your teen make a conscious effort to stop and think through the situation. Could the anger stem from a misunderstanding?
- Problem solving techniques can help your teen address a problem by identifying it and then trying to work toward a solution. Warn your teen that it may not be a quick solution.
- Suggest "alone time" for your teen. This can help him or her manage stress and reduce feelings of anger and frustration.
- Some common stress-reducing alone activities:
    Meditation
    Writing feelings and thoughts in a journal
    Listening to music
    Exercising
    Taking a walk

What *Not* to Do:

Yell, curse, or name-call:

There's no excuse for abuse—not by your child and not by you. In the same way that playing the victim role is no excuse for your child to abuse someone else, your child abusing you does not excuse *your* yelling, cursing, or name-calling. Being verbally abusive to your child only makes things worse, both in the short-term when the argument escalates, and in the long-term when your child's behavior does not change and your relationship becomes strained.

Threaten with consequences:

It is always most effective to avoid threatening your child with specific consequences in the heat of the moment. For example, saying, "If you do not stop, I'm taking your computer for 3 days" is not likely to get your child to suddenly stop yelling and retreat to his room. Instead, it will upset your child even more and keep the argument going. What is more effective is to say, "If you choose not to go to your room and calm down, there will be a consequence later" and then walk away.

Attempt to control your child:

This is one of the biggest stumbling blocks for parents. We hear from parents every day who, without realizing it, are trying to control their children. I think this is due, in part, to some common confusion about accountability and what that really means. Holding your child accountable does not result in a child who is obedient 100 percent of the time. It does not mean that your child will always choose to follow the rules even if you give him consequences consistently when he misbehaves. Accountability means that you set the rules and the limits, and you provide a consequence when your child decides to break the rules—period. The goal is not to prevent your child from ever breaking the rules. You're not a puppeteer; you're a limit-setter. Let your child make his own choice. Limits and rules were literally made to be crossed and broken because that is how we, as humans, learn about consequences and accountability.

Another way to look at accountability is this: If your child does not follow the rules, someone will find out and there will be a "price" to pay, a "cost" for his poor choice in the form of the temporary loss of a privilege he enjoys. When a child experiences this unpleasant outcome, he can use that information to help him think about things next time he is considering breaking the rules. He will learn to ask himself, "Is it worth it?" as he is making his choices in the future.

Get physical:

This often goes hand in hand with trying to control your child. Your child didn't turn the X-box off when you told him to, so you try to take the controller or the console itself in the heat of your argument when everyone's emotions are running high. Or, your child threatens to leave the house when she is angry so you try to physically keep her in the home by blocking her path or holding her back physically. Let me be clear: it is *not* a good idea to get physical with your child, first and foremost because it shows your child that the way to gain control of a situation is to use physical force. Secondly, you run the risk of escalating the entire situation. Remember how we talked about that natural urge to fight back? Well, I'm sure you know that urge is very real for your teen as well. I've heard many stories from parents about their kids striking back in response to the parent getting physical with them first. Do not risk it. *It is not worth it.*

Try to "win":

If you're one of those parents who already knows that the way to gain control of an argument with your child is to walk away and calm yourself down, then you can disregard this point. Realize that if you continue to try to "win" every battle with your child, you will lose "the war." To be honest, I do not like using "war" and "battle" comparisons because it makes it sound as if your child is your enemy. It may feel like it more often than not, but remember, your child is not really your enemy—he is a kid in need of some more effective problem-solving skills.

What I have found is that the goal for most parents I talk to is to raise their child to be respectful, accountable adults that can make it on their own in this world. If that is the case for you, then think carefully about the battles along the way. James Lehman says, "Pick your battles, and be prepared to win the ones you pick." This means asking yourself "Is it worth it?" before you go charging into "battle" with your child. It does not mean to "win" by out-yelling your child—it means that you succeed by using effective strategies that are going to help you achieve that long-term goal.

What TO Do: Try These Techniques Instead

Pick your battles and consider walking away:

As mentioned above, ask yourself if it is worth it to deal with this issue. Does it need to be dealt with *right now*? Should you take some time to calm down before you address it with your child? Are your buttons being pushed? Think about the situation carefully and allow some time for things to cool down. You can address it later if you still feel the issue is important after you've thought it through.

Use a business-like tone:

James Lehman talks about the concept of treating your family like a business in the Total Transformation program. You're the CEO of your "family business," so when things are turbulent, remember to address your child in the same tone with which a professionally mannered boss would address an employee with a performance issue. Stay calm and neutral, and stick to the facts.

Self-disclosure:

Let your child know you're having a hard time communicating with them in the moment. It is perfectly okay to say things like, "It is really hard for me to listen and talk to you when you're screaming at me," or "When you scream at me, I do not really feel like helping you." This is a simple way to set a limit with your child and let them know their behavior isn't working.

Challenge your child's thinking:

When I say "challenge" here I do not mean invite your child to keep sparring with you by saying things like, "You think you're pretty tough, big guy!?" What I mean is to point out that his behavior is ineffective. Say to your child, "I know you want to go to the mall, but talking to me like that is not going to get you what you want," or "I get that you're angry, but screaming at me isn't going to get me to let you play your video games before your homework is done."

Last but not least, one of the single best ways to teach kids is by example. Role modeling is one of the key components of teaching kids how to behave. I've said it before, and I will say it again: If you do not want your child to yell at you, do not yell at him. If you do not want your child to curse, do not curse. As James Lehman says, "You've got to model the behavior you want to see from your child."

Ask yourself, "What have I been modeling?"

The way you speak to a child can have a great impact on what a child may think is acceptable behavior. For example, if you are too loud and utilize anger to quiet a child down, then he or she may think that until you aren't that angry, that it is okay to behave that way until a reaction similar to the one described above is demonstrated. A quiet but firm demeanor may elicit a response that demonstrates that you have control of the situation. Anger does not necessarily mean that you have the respect of the child; rather, it can demonstrate to a child that you do not mean business until you are angry.

Not only do kids become less responsive to angry parents, but also anger itself can manifest in a contagious manner. For example, when someone gets angry with you, you yourself can find yourself in a raging manner. Sometimes you may feel the need to yell back. When a parent demonstrates anger towards a teenager, the teenager may also demonstrate it back.

Given the situation described above, a teenager may not respond back respectfully if anger has been the way you have communicated with your teen during their upbringing. Be persistent with your child. It takes more then one attempt to undo bad habits and for all family members to adjust to new relational rules.

Take a personal inventory:

Parents, for the most part, have the best interest of their children. However, there are times in which we do not treat the child with the respect that they deserve. This can be intentionally done or unintentionally. This can lead to an angry teen.

Have you made your teenager feel unwanted, controlled, manipulated or ignored? If you think you have contributed to your child feeling frustrated, just keep in mind that no parent is perfect. With humility, there is always a chance to change prior behavior that may have you feeling this way. The main thing to remember is to keep the communication lines with your teenager open.

Sometimes you may need to show tough love:

Tough love is often a necessary tool when parents find their children disrespectful and angry and refusing to change in spite of your kind efforts. By setting rules for the teenager, such as yelling and verbally attacking will not be tolerated, and enforcing consequences for the bad behavior. Consequences should be impactful to the teenager, such as removing a privilege. A privilege can be as simple as driving or removing personal devices from their accessibility such as their cellphone or gaming system. Be consistent in the punishment and do not fold in. The result will demonstrate a more controlled teenager who loves themselves and those around him. This will also help them create a healthy foundation for rewarding relationships.

Encourage Appropriate Communication:

The most effective way to deal with anger and rebellious behavior is to have teenagers appropriately communicate their feelings of disapproval and resentment. Encourage them to express and explain negative feelings, sources of anger, and their opinions—that is, what angers them, what we do that they do not like, what they disapprove of. If a teenager expresses emotions appropriately, in a normal tone of voice, she should not be viewed as rude or disrespectful. This is an appropriate expression of anger, and the youngster should not be reprimanded or punished. In other words, allow teenagers to complain, disagree, or disapprove, provided they are not sarcastic, flippant, or nasty. Remember, though, that allowing a child to shout, swear, or be fresh does not teach effective communication of emotions.

Listen. If the teenager is complaining about excessive restrictions, punishments, or other things that she does not like, *listen.* Try to understand her feelings. If the complaints are realistic, see if something can be worked out and resolved, or if a compromise can be achieved.

Avoid Excessive Negative Attention:

It is a mistake to pay more attention to what the child is doing wrong—his failures, mistakes, misbehaviors—than to what he is doing right—his successes, achievements, good behaviors. When you go to bed at night, review the day you have had with your child. Have you spent as much time during the day looking at his appropriate behaviors as you have looking at his inappropriate actions? You should avoid using punishment as a primary method of control. Instead, substitute positive consequences, which place the emphasis on good behavior rather than on bad behavior. Eliminate verbal punishment (hollering, putting down the adolescent, name-calling, excessive criticism), and use reward as a disciplinary tactic. Emphasize successes, accomplishments, achievements, and good behaviors. Pay more attention to normal good behavior and be positive.

Constant nagging of a teenager will certainly result in a buildup of anger, resentment, and aggressive behaviors.

Try Not to React to Passive-Aggressive Behavior:

Some of the opposition, stubbornness, resistance, and other passive-aggressive maneuvers of teenagers are designed to express anger and/or to get a reaction from the parents. Ignoring this behavior is often an effective way to reduce it.

Some ways of dealing with this passive-aggressive behavior will result in the development of more anger, while others will help deflate the anger balloon. For example, a child is told to set the table for dinner. While setting the table, she mumbles under her breath and every now and then you hear comments like, "They think I'm a slave. I want to go live at Grandma's, where I'm appreciated." Along with the mumbling, she is angrily tossing ice in the glasses and banging down the plates and silverware. This teenager is annoyed because she feels she has better things to do than set the table. Her mumbling and other actions are passive-aggressive maneuvers to express her anger and resentment. These behaviors are releasing anger and letting air out of the anger balloon. If you react to her mumbling by criticizing or scolding, you will be putting more air back into the balloon—that is, the anger that was initially released by the child's complaining and defiance will be offset by a buildup of additional aggressive feelings. By using the consequence of ignoring her, this additional buildup of anger can be eliminated.

There are several things that must be kept in mind when using this consequence, and there are a few different ways to ignore the behavior. In general, if you ask a teenager to do something and he is doing it, although complaining the whole time, ignore his complaints since he is doing what you asked.

Avoid Random Discipline:

Parents often discipline after the fact. I call this random discipline. They set a rule and wait for the adolescent to break it before they decide upon a consequence. To teenagers, the concept of fairness is extremely important. If they are disciplined in this fashion, they may frequently feel unjustly treated. In addition, random discipline often makes teenagers feel that others are responsible for what has happened to them and anger is apt to develop. You should spell out the rules and consequences for your child's behavior at the same time. The most important part of this process is not the rule, but the consequence. Put the responsibility for what happens to the child squarely on his or her shoulders.

Do Not Get Into a Power Struggle:

You tell the adolescent to clean his room and he refuses. Then you threaten, "You had better clean it, or you're not going out on Saturday."

He replies, "You can't make me clean it and I'm going out on Saturday, anyway." Then you say something, he says something, you both begin to shout, and a full-blown power struggle has developed. This is a good way to generate anger in your child.

When possible, avoid battles and power struggles, which only lead to a buildup of anger. At times, it may be better to have the child experience the consequence of his behavior rather than to win the battle and get him to do what you want. If you try to win each fight, you may battle the child throughout adolescence, and will probably end up losing the war.

Tommy was an angry teenager." There were lots of holes in my bedroom wall," said 21-year-old Tommy, recalling the "superhuman strength" that sent his VCR clear across the room. "I would say I was a little on edge." For Tommy, who also struggled with an eating disorder in his teens, anger was a way release the pressure of high school. "I didn't develop appropriate coping mechanisms," Tommy said. Tommy is now a junior at a university in New Jersey. He patched up his relationships with his parents and the holes in his wall and left his teenage years behind. He credits talk therapy for his victory over anger, as well as medication that helps decrease his anxiety.

Other Methods for Handling Anger and Increasing Self-Esteem

Ask the child "I am worth it" questions?

1. **T** what are your thoughts and feelings?
2. **I** Is it an important situation?
3. **A** Are my thoughts and feelings appropriate?
4. **M** is the situation modifiable?
5. **A** is it worth to take anger?

If you answered three questions with a "no," then it would be helpful for you to take an anger management course.

If you answered three questions with a "yes," then you might want to do something about the situation in a respectful, logical way.

Do you lose your temper and wonder why? Are there days when you feel like you just wake up angry?

Your body is constantly changing, and one of these changes is due to hormones that can cause symptoms such as mood swings and emotions that are relatively confusing. Other components can be stress related. For example, you have time sensitive tasks that you cannot seem to complete that are making you feel like you are under an immense pressure. These individuals may find themselves getting angry more often and more easily. Other aspects can be the individual's personality. There are individuals who may find themselves more impulsive and tend to lose control. Last but not least, role models also play a crucial role in the way we behave. There may be other influential family members who reacted a certain way and we associate that anger with an appropriate response to certain situations.

No matter what pushes your buttons, one thing is certain — you are sure to get angry. Anger is a normal emotion, and there's nothing wrong with feeling mad. What counts is how we handle it (and ourselves) when we are angry.

TOOLS TO TAME A TEMPER:
SELF-AWARENESS & SELF-CONTROL

Managing your anger can be extremely challenging. By practicing self-awareness and self-control you can control the powerful emotion known as anger. However, these skills take time to develop.

Self-awareness is the ability to notice what you're feeling and thinking, and why. Little kids aren't very aware of what they feel; they just act it out in their behavior. That is why you see them having tantrums when He is mad. But teens have the mental ability to be self-aware. When you get angry, take a moment to notice what you're feeling and thinking.

Self-control is all about thinking before you act. It puts some precious seconds or minutes between feeling a strong emotion and taking an action you'll regret.

Together, self-awareness and self-control allow you to have more choice about how to act when you're feeling an intense emotion like anger.

Getting Ready to Make a Change

Self-reflection is looking closely at the way you have been reacting when you get mad. Do you throw things, kick or punch walls, break stuff? Hit someone, hurt yourself, or push and shove others around?

For most people who have trouble harnessing a hot temper, reacting like this is not what they want. They feel ashamed by their behavior and do not think it reflects the real them, their best selves.

Change can be done by anyone, but only when an individual is ready to do so. If you want to change how you're handling emotions such as anger think about what you'll gain from that change. Remembering why you want to make the change can help.

It can also help to remind yourself that making a change takes time, practice, and patience. It won't happen all at once. Managing anger is about developing new skills and new responses.

The Five-Step Approach to Managing Anger

The Five-step approach to managing anger is a great way of handling the way you react to situations. This approach is considered problem solving because your reaction will be managed to a situation that once makes you angry. You will also find yourself looking at what your options are and see what choice is best for you.

Each step involves asking yourself a couple of questions, and then answering them based on your particular situation.

Here's what to do:

- **Identify the problem (self-awareness).** Start by noticing what you're angry about and why. Put into words what is making you upset so you can act rather than react.

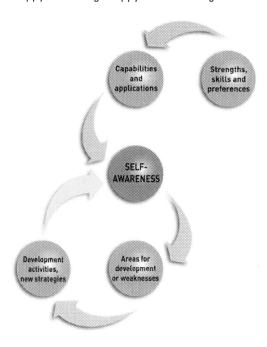

- **_Ask yourself:_** What is got me angry? What am I feeling and why? You can do this either in your mind or out loud, but it needs to be clear and specific. For example: "I'm really angry at Mom because she won't let me go to the party until I clean my room. It is not fair!" Your feeling is anger, and you're feeling angry because you might not get to go to the party.

- Notice that this is not the same as saying, "Mom's so unfair to me." That statement does not identify the specific problem (that you can't go to the party until you clean your room) and it does not say how you are feeling (angry).

- **Think of potential solutions before responding (self-control).** This is where you stop for a minute to give yourself time to manage your anger. It is also where you start thinking of how you might react — but without reacting yet.

Ask yourself: What can I do? Think of at least three things.

Consider the consequences of each solution (think it through). This is where you think about what is likely to result from each of the different reactions you came up with.

(a) I could yell at Mom and throw a fit. (b) I could clean my room and then ask if I could go to the party. (c) I could sneak out to the party anyway.

- **Consider the consequences of each solution (think it through).** This is where you think about what is likely to result from each of the different reactions you came up with.

Ask yourself: What will happen for each one of these options? For example:

(a) Yelling at your mom may get you in worse trouble or even grounded. (b) Cleaning your room takes work and you may get to the party late (but maybe that adds to your mystique). With this option, you get to go to the party *and* your room's clean so you do not have to worry about it for a while. (c) Sneaking out may seem like a real option in the heat of anger. But when you really think it through, it is pretty unlikely you'd get away with being gone for hours with no one noticing. And when you do get caught — look out!

- **Make a decision (pick one of your options).** This is where you take action by choosing one of the three things you could do. Look at the list and pick the one that is likely to be most effective.

- *Ask yourself:* What will happen for each one of these options. Make a decision (pick one of your options). This is where you take action by choosing one of the three things you could do. Look at the list and pick the one that is likely to be most effective.

- *Ask yourself:* What is my best choice? By the time you've thought it through, you're probably past yelling at your mom, which is a knee-jerk response. You may have also decided that sneaking out is too risky. Neither of these options is likely to get you to the party. So option (b) probably seems like the best choice.

Once you choose your solution, then it is time to act.

Check your progress. After you've acted and the situation is over, spend some time thinking about how it went.

Ask yourself: How did I do? Did things work out as I expected? If not, why not? Am I satisfied with the choice I made? Taking some time to reflect on how things worked out after it is all over is a very important step. It helps you learn about yourself and it allows you to test which problem-solving approaches work best in different situations.

Give yourself a pat on the back if the solution you chose worked out well. If it didn't, go back through the five steps and see if you can figure out why.

These five steps are pretty simple when you're calm, but are much tougher to work through when you're angry or sad. So it helps to practice over and over again.

Other Ways to Manage Anger

The five-step approach is good when you're in a particular situation. That is, a situation that got you mad and you need to decide what action to take. But other things can help you manage anger too.

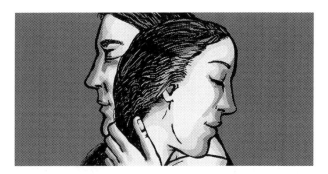

Try these things even if you're not mad right now to help prevent angry feelings from building up inside.

The five-step approach is good when you're in a particular situation. That is, a situation that got you mad and you need to decide what action to take. But other things can help you manage anger too.

Try these things even if you're not mad right now to help prevent angry feelings from building up inside.

- Go for a walk/run, work out, or go play a sport.
- Listen to music (with your headphones on).
- Write down your thoughts and emotions. You can write things in lots of ways; for example, in a journal or as your own poetry or song lyrics.
- Draw. Scribbling, doodling, or sketching your thoughts or feelings might help too.
- Meditate or practice deep breathing This one works best if you do it regularly, as it is more of an overall stress management technique that can help you use self-control when you're mad. If you do this regularly, you'll find that anger is less likely to build up.
- Talk about your feelings with someone you trust.
- - Distract yourself. If you find yourself stewing about something and just can't seem to let go, it can help to do something that will get your mind past what is bugging you — watch TV, read, or go to the movies.

These ideas can be helpful for two reasons:

1. **They help you cool down when you feel like your anger might explode.** When you need to cool down, do one or more of the activities in the list above. Think of these, as alternatives

247

to taking an action you'll regret, such as yelling at someone. Some of them, like writing down feelings, can help you release tension and begin the thinking process at the same time.

2. **They help you manage anger in general.** What if there's no immediate problem to solve — you simply need to shift into a better mood? Sometimes when you're angry, you just need to stop dwelling on how mad you are.

When to Ask for Extra Help

Sometimes anger is a sign that more is going on. People who have frequent trouble with anger, who get in fights or arguments, who get punished, who have life situations that give them reason to often be angry may need special help to get a problem with anger under control.

Tell your parents, a teacher, a counselor, or another adult you trust if any of these things have been happening:

- The feelings of anger are harboring and will not go away whether its from the past or present.
- You feel irritable, grumpy, or in a bad mood more often than not.
- You feel consistent anger or rage at yourself
- You feel anger that lasts for days or makes you want to hurt yourself or someone else.
- You are often getting into fights or arguments.

These could be signs of depression or something else — and you should not have to handle that alone. Anger is a strong emotion. It can feel overwhelming at times. Learning how to deal with strong emotions — without losing control — is part of becoming more mature. It takes a little effort, a little practice, and a little patience, but you can get there if you want to.

Communication

As we said earlier, communication is key. Communication and understanding what others say is extremely important in general and especially crucial during the teen years. If people did not communicate, we would not be able to know what others wanted, what to do or where to go. If you are in class, and you do not understand something the teacher is saying, you ask a question. Then you listen to the explanation and hopefully understand what you did not understand earlier. Communication is also important if you have pent-up emotions.

If the feelings are bad or sad, and you do not express them, they can start to make you feel disagreeable and/or distraught. If the feelings are happy, they might make you overly spunky or giddy. If you have pent-up feelings, talk to someone about them.

During great disturbances in your life, such as a move, school change or parents' divorce, it is a good idea to talk to people so you can deal with your feelings and move on, making the best of the situation. If you do not want to talk to your parents, try your friends or siblings, or else a counselor, therapist or doctor. **The crucial thing is to express your feelings**. Otherwise, these Feelings can get stuck inside your head, circle around and never get out, and lead to problems with focus, sleep and relaxation.

Communication involves talking and listening. They go hand in hand. Relationships are two-sided; each person has a responsibility to make themselves heard and to hear other people. If you are always listening, or if you are always talking, the relationship is not balanced.

Remember to express yourself. In the end, you will feel better. Signs of good communication include the ability to express your needs, wants and feelings. Think about what you want from the communication; define specific goals and a specific message. Decide the best outcome you would be satisfied with, and work to achieve your goal. A key to successful communication is not to blame the other person. Use "I" statements instead of "you" statements. Express how you feel instead of blaming the other person. Setbacks may occur, but keep working at it!

Communication Skills

You can probably think of at least one conversation in which you felt completely connected to the person you were talking with -- and at least one conversation you left feeling dissatisfied because of a lack of understanding between you and the other person. Although you can't guarantee that every conversation will be great, you can learn skills to make communication a bit easier and more satisfying. Even if you are already a good communicator, consciously thinking about what you do to communicate well can help you to improve your skills and use them even when you're upset or unsure of what to say. This article covers some basic communication tips and strategies to improve your communication skills, as well as ideas for preparing for particularly difficult communication tasks.

More Key Ideas for Communication

What a conversation is like depends greatly on who is involved. Clearly, a conversation with your teacher tends to be very different than a conversation with your best friend. **The other person (or people) in the conversation is your audience, and being conscious of your audience can remind you of your purpose.** While these words sound a bit like something you might hear in English class, keeping them in mind can help you focus on the important parts of a conversation. For instance, consider the following conversation: Teen: "Hey, can I go to Jamie's tomorrow night?" Parent: "Will Jamie's parents be there? Who else will be there?" One possible response is for the teen to get annoyed with the parent for asking questions; another is for the teen to answer the questions or explain more about why he wants to go to Jamie's house. Most teens get frustrated with their parents; it is completely normal. However, it is also not particularly helpful when you're asking for permission to do something. Keeping in mind his audience, the above teen might catch himself prior to responding with anger to the parent's questions. After all, the purpose of this conversation is obtaining permission to go to Jamie's house; refusing to answer the parent's questions is unlikely to elicit that permission, which defeats the purpose. **Paying attention to your audience and purpose does not mean you can't express your emotions,** but it is a reminder to yourself about how to express those emotions in a positive and constructive manner. Purpose may not matter as much when you're talking with a friend, but it can be important when you have a conversation you want to keep on track and lead to a specific point. If you're worried about a particular conversation, remembering the purpose can help to deal with some of that anxiety and make the conversation easier.

Improving your communication skills takes some planning. Think about how you can prepare:

- **Pre-Conversation**
    - **Cool off.** It is good to feel your emotions but not be too emotional. Emotions can be unproductive when they get in the way of rationality. Especially when people just find out something upsetting or a lot of stress has suddenly built up, they have a biological fight or flight reaction and can't reason as effectively. **If you are really emotional, take some time to cool off.** A good test is if you can imagine yourself listening to the other person's perspective without blowing up. If you can do that, go ahead and talk. If you can't, the conversation will most likely be unproductive, and it is worth a couple hours to calm down.

- **Know what is important to you.** A lot of times people initiate tough conversations without really reflecting beforehand what is important to them. Take time to write down the three or four things that you most want the other person to understand. The challenge is writing down what is important to you without using the other person in your statement. Below are several examples:

- o "Having my own space is really important to me." (Instead of "You need to get off my back all the time!")
- o "It is really important to me that I make my own decisions." (Instead of "You need to stop telling me what to do!")
- o "It is important to me that I feel respected." (Instead of "You need to stop insulting me!")

When you know what is important to you and can frame it in a way that isn't threatening, the other person will be much more likely to listen to you.

- **Guess what is important to them.**

Even though it might be hard to admit, the other person has things that are important to them, too. It is often important to parents that they know their child is safe. It is important to some significant others that they get their space or that they feel loved. The faster you understand what is important to the other person, the better you can empathize with him or her and the more productive your conversation will be.

Again, write down what you think is important to them without using yourself in the statement. Below are several examples.

- It is important to him that he knows his children are safe. (Instead of "He wants me to check in with him every 5 minutes.")
- It is important to him that he gets sleep at night because it is important that he does well at work in the morning. (Instead of "He wants me to turn my music down at night".)

Even if you're wrong, thinking about what is important to them before the conversation will make it easier to listen during the conversation.

During the Conversation

- **Listen -- actively!** Communication isn't only about telling other people what you think; it also involves understanding what ideas and thoughts other people have. If in a conversation you find yourself constantly thinking, "What will I say next?" try stepping back a bit and just focus on what the person currently talking is saying. **One way to check if you're really listening to the other person is to try to paraphrase (restate in your own words) what she or he said.** For instance, consider the conversation below. Jamie: "I can't stand Morgan. She is so screwed up!" Pat: "Wow, sounds like something is going on between you two. Did something happen?" Jamie knows that Pat was really listening, and this invites Jamie to confirm what Pat said and expand on the problems with the friendship. This sort of paraphrasing can be useful for making sure you understand what was said and also for giving you some time to think about your response. Active listening also involves little things like acknowledging what a person has said and asking more about things that interest you. **The more you listen, the more the other person will listen to you.** If what you say might offend the other person, be prepared even to

Listen before you are listened to. Be the example of how you would want the other person to react to what you were telling them. Be patient. When he or she seems to have finished, ask if he or she is done. If is the person is finished, say, "What you've said is really important, and I really want to hear everything you have to say. If you're done for now, can I say what is been on my mind for about 10 minutes? Will you promise to listen?" People tend to mirror each other in conflict. If you listen to them, they will often treat you similarly. And the more you both understand each other, the more productive your conversation will be.

- **Make eye contact.** All non-verbal gestures are equally important! Imagine conducting a conversation with someone who won't look at you, or stares at the TV, or raises his or her eyebrows in a look of skepticism every time you speak. Even if the person carried on a perfectly normal conversation otherwise, the communication would probably be worse than if he or she used appropriate non-verbal communication. **Non-verbal communication involves things that might seem minor, such as making eye contact and focusing your attention on the person who's speaking,** but it can be vital to having a conversation that feels respectful on both sides. Paying attention to someone else's non-verbal communication can also give you clues as to whether the person understands what you're saying. Using good non-verbal communication shows you respect the other person enough to listen to what they are saying--an important aspect of any conversation.

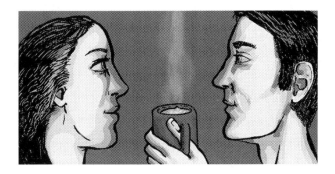

- **Express your views.** Be respectful, but do not be afraid. It is easy to just agree with everyone else or to decide to stay quiet rather than talk about what you're thinking, but in the end, this can often leave you frustrated. It also means that you aren't really communicating! If you're honest about what you think and feel, people will generally have more respect for you, and they will certainly be able to understand you better. As you begin expressing your views, you might feel uncertain, but try starting off with small things. **The more you express your views, the easier it gets.**

- **Use "I" statements, especially when talking about something negative.** Using "I" statements can help turn an argument into a productive discussion rather than a shouting match. It also makes expressing your views easier because you're just talking about yourself. What is an "I" statement? Check out A and B, and guess which one is an example of an "I" statement. A: "You hurt my feelings. You know I wanted to come. You didn't have to go without me." B: "I feel hurt that you did not wait to go with me. I told you I wanted to come." B is an example of an "I" statement. The speaker clearly expressed what she felt and accepted responsibility for the feeling. In A, the speaker is blaming the person she is talking to for the feeling of anger. If you've ever been blamed for something, you probably know that it does not feel very good and tends to put people on the defensive. "I" statements let you take responsibility for what you feel and are less likely to make the other person feel defensive. Combined with honesty, they can be extremely helpful for dealing with conflicts. You wrote down what was important to you before the conversation, right? Now express what you want to say just how you wrote it. Start by saying what is really important to you and how that need is not being fulfilled. For instance, "It is really important to me that I feel respected. When you ignore me every day when I come home, I do not feel respected." Or "It is really important to me that I feel like I can make my own decisions.

When you do not listen to my opinions, I do not feel like I have control over my own life." Other people can empathize with what is important to you, but it is harder to listen to someone blaming you.

- **Understand everyone's point of view.** Where you are coming from and where the other person is coming from? Considering what causes you to feel the way you do can help you to understand why someone else feels differently, and it can also help you express your feelings more clearly. It also allows you to disagree with another person while still respecting their position. For instance, the example below shows how a person's point of view might affect how they think. Taylor: "I do not want to go to school today." Dana: "But it is track and field day; it is always so much fun! We have no real classes and tons of parents come and watch the races." Taylor: "Yeah, but I do not like competing with everyone else. And my parents can't even come." Dana and Taylor are both talking about the same event, but their perspectives are very different. In more complicated cases, a person might have an opinion because of how she or he was raised or because of his or her personal beliefs. Acknowledging the person's feelings and being respectful of those feelings can keep a conversation from degenerating. Additionally, keeping track of why you hold certain beliefs can allow you to tell those reasons to others, making your beliefs clearer and easier to understand.

- **Set ground rules.** Think about informal rules you want to make before the conversation that will make it go more smoothly. Maybe you're afraid that what you say isn't going to be kept secret. Maybe you're afraid you're going to start crying and not be able to listen. If this is the case, use the time right before the conversation to say: "Before we start, I just want to make sure that everything that is said here is kept in confidence, is that OK with you?" Or "Before we start, I just want to say if I lose it and start crying or yelling, I will step out of the room for 10 minutes, and then we can continue. Does that sound good to you?" Give the other person a chance to ask for ground rules, too. The more safe both of you feel to express your feelings and ideas, the more productive your conversation will be.

- **Do not react -- Reflect.** The biggest danger to avoid in a tough conversation is the back and forth. Everyone's experienced the back and forth: right after one person says something, the other person reacts, and the conversation escalates and goes nowhere. Here's how to avoid it. When the other person makes a statement, do not react. Instead reflect, summarize what they are saying and say it back to them. If

  They say, "I can't believe you are telling me this now!" do not offer an explanation right away. Instead say, "You're really upset that I waited to tell you this." If you immediately explain why you didn't tell them earlier, the other person will probably be so upset that they won't hear you anyway. But **if you reflect back to the other person the content of what he or she said, then he or she will feel understood and will be much more likely to listen to you.** Keep reflecting until the other person is done. Be patient. Then ask this person if he or she will listen to you.

- **Be Specific.** When you and the other person decide how you want to move forward, be specific about what you both will do. A lot of times, people make vague agreements like "I will give you more space" or "We'll spend more time together." Instead, make agreements that are specific actions. For example, "When your door is closed, I will knock and wait for an answer before I come in." Or, "Wednesdays at 7 p.m., we will go have coffee." These agreements are easier to keep and easier to check. Back to top

Post-Conversation

1. **Keep your end of the agreement.** Relationships are built on trust, but trust can't be built in an hour conversation. The first step to rebuilding trust with a person is showing you're committed by following through on your agreement. If you care about that relationship, make sure you put time into doing what

you said you would do. If you do this, your conversation will be less difficult next time.

2. **Reflect.** I know you wish this were the last tough conversation you will ever have. But chances are, you'll have more tough conversations: if not with that person, with many other people in the future. Take a half hour to reflect on the conversation.
   - What worked well in that conversation?
   - Where did you run into pitfalls?
   - Do you need to work on listening?
   - Do you need to work on saying things without blaming?
   - What might you do next time you have a tough conversation?

Preparing for a Tough Conversation

Sometimes you know a particular conversation will be difficult. Maybe you're worried about breaking up with your significant other or confronting a friend about his or her betrayal. Maybe you simply are nervous about presenting a new idea to a parent or teacher. Whatever the situation, preparing ahead of time can make the final conversation easier. One way to make things easier is to think out what you want to say ahead of time. In the case of presenting a new idea, you might try presenting it to someone else first and getting his or her feedback on what you said. If it is something more private, you could try writing out your feelings and thoughts first to help you organize what you want to say, as well as clarify how you feel.

Simply thinking through what you would like to say in the conversation and what your purpose is can make it easier for you when you're actually having the conversation.

These steps can also make you less nervous or worried before the conversation, making it more likely that the conversation will go well. Even if you do not feel comfortable talking about the specific subject that the conversation will be about, try talking to a friend about your nervousness to help you feel more comfortable. Depending on what type of conversation you're having, **you might find it helpful to tell the person you're talking to that you're nervous** or concerned. For instance, if you were to talk to a friend about an eating disorder, you might start the conversation with "I do not really know how to bring this up, and I know it might be uncomfortable to talk about, but I'm really concerned that you haven't eaten lunch in the past two weeks." This tells the other person how you're feeling but also demonstrates that you think the conversation is important enough to move beyond your discomfort and worry. This sort of disclaimer might not be appropriate when you are trying to impress someone (such as in a job interview, where it is best to appear poised and composed even if you feel nervous) but it can be very helpful in other situations. Finally, if the conversation is weighing on your mind considerably, you might try distracting yourself for a little while. Taking a few deep breaths and clearing your mind can help quell physical symptoms of nervousness. Jogging or doing anything physical can also help you to shed nervous fidgeting and give your mind a break from worry. For more ideas on how to relax, check out this page about stress. When we communicate with another person, what we say is not necessarily the most important part of our message. Our body language and our tone can say so much more than our words. Through successful communication, you develop a sense of trust, the second building block of The ABCs.

MODULE 10

Punishment vs. Discipline

How do you define discipline? What does discipline mean to you? What is the goal of discipline? What is it we hope to accomplish when we discipline children?

We often hear people say, "Spare the Rod, Spoil the Child," when referring to discipline. What does that mean?

Discipline comes from the word "disciple" which means to teach. Children are expected to behave a certain way yet they are not told what is expected of them. The rod that is so often mentioned does not mean that you have to spank the child. Rather, the rod refers to the staff the shepherds used to gently move the sheep in the direction they wanted them to go.

That is exactly what is meant when discipline and children are discussed.

The goal is to help children move in the direction that parents think is right and appropriate.

Another goal is to help children reach the level of self-discipline. Parents are not always going to be with the child, and you want children to "behave," whether you are present or absent.

When should discipline occur? Before the behavior/misdeed? After the behavior/misdeed?

Discipline should occur before the behavior/misdeed. The critical issue is teaching the child about acceptable behaviors so he/she will know in advance how to behave. This does not negate that at times children will misbehave. The difference is they will know internally that they are doing something wrong and move to correct the behavior sometimes even before parents can intervene.

Discipline Relates to Self-Concept:

Appropriate disciplinary measures fuels positive self-concept; aids in mental stability; encourages healthy growth and development.

Remember the rights of children? More specifically, to maintenance: food, clothing, shelter; to protection; to emotional security; to education; to medical care; to privacy; etc.

What is the relationship between these rights and discipline?

When disciplining children bear in mind the Objective is to protect rather than violate those rights.

PUNISHMENT

How is punishment similar or different from discipline? What does punishment mean to you? How do you define it?

Punishment is a negative consequence; it occurs after a behavior; it aims to stop the behavior or is a deterrent.

What are some examples of punishment?

```




```

Do these protect the rights of children? Do they engender positive self-concept?

Why punishment doesn't work and what does:

- ✓ Punishment can be punitive and may increase rage, revenge, defiance, and guilt, while decreasing introspection.
- ✓ Deprivation is easy but not always appropriate.
- ✓ Hitting increases guilt for the parent while teaching the child that when one is angry, one hits.

Discipline by appropriate consequences:

- Teaches alternatives to punishment
- Increases children's understanding of appropriate behavior
- Corrects misbehavior and discourages repetition of misbehavior
- Does not use punitive statements, is relevant to the action, and makes sense to the child
- Uses "I" messages to communicate anger and disappointment while giving the child a chance to make amends
- May put the child in a position of problem solver thereby building upon problem solving skills

NOTES:

WHY NOT TO USE PHYSICAL FORCE
WHEN YOU'RE CHILD MISBEHAVES:

- ✓ Even if hitting her makes her stop misbehaving for that minute, it teaches her it's OK to hit and yell when upset and angry
- ✓ Physical punishment, even the lightest slap, can harm a child
- ✓ Hitting teaches the child fear rather than self-control
- ✓ Hitting teaches the child that it is OK to hurt and be hurt by those you love
- ✓ Hitting teaches that problems get resolved through violence

ALTERNATIVES TO HITTING CHILDREN:

- ✓ STOP AND THINK! STEP BACK OR SIT DOWN
- ✓ TAKE A FEW DEEP BREATHS—EXHALE SLOWLY
- ✓ COUNT TO 20 OR 100—WHATEVER IT TAKES YOU TO RELAX
- ✓ PHONE A FRIEND OR RELATIVE—TALK ABOUT ANYTHING OR ASK FOR HELP
- ✓ WRITE A LIST ABOUT ALL THE THINGS YOU LIKE ABOUT YOUR CHILDABOUT YOURSELF
- ✓ PUT ON A FAVORITE RECORD, CD, OR RADIO STATIONREAD A MAGAZINE OR BOOK
- ✓ EXPLAIN TO THE CHILD WHY YOU ARE ANGRY IF THE CHILD IS OLD ENOUGH TO UNDERSTAND
- ✓ ASK YOURSELF WHY YOU ARE GOING TO SMACK YOUR CHILD
- ✓ ASK YOURSELF WILL SMACKING YOUR CHILD MAKE THINGS BETTER

NOTES:

CONSEQUENCES OF HITTING:

The goal in raising children is to enable them, first, to discover whom they want to be, and then to become people who can be satisfied with themselves and their way of life. Eventually, they ought to be able to do in their lives whatever seems important, desirable, and worthwhile to them to do; to develop relationships with other people that are constructive, satisfying, mutually enriching; and to bear up well under the stresses and hardships they will unavoidably encounter during their life. In this regard, parents are not just foremost teachers, they are those by whom and through whom children orient themselves with the world around them.

Children have a need for attachment and parents can build on their need in order to promote the child's self-control and a lasting inner commitment to be a discipline person. Discipline cannot be forced on another person. Any discipline worth acquiring cannot be beaten into anyone; indeed, such effort is contrary to the very ideas of healthy growth and development. Hitting teaches children fear, poor self-concept, feelings of revenge, and the idea that it's okay to hit those you love. It does not teach children to obey rules, be careful, make wise choices, or have inner control.

Hitting, even the threat of hitting, often teaches children fear. Children who learn to fear their parents often learn to fear other adults as well. The sheer difference in size between parents and children can be frightening. When parents threaten or use their physical superiority as a form of punishment, young children realize there is no way they could ever win. Their safety is literally at the mercy of the angry parent.

The self-concept and self-esteem of children develop from how they are treated. Children who are constantly threatened or hit learn that they are not worthy people, are not loved, and are not wanted. Nobody ever feels good after being hit. The more frequent the hitting, the more constant the feelings of inadequacy. In addition, many studies indicate children who have been hit exhibit a high degree of anxiety as well as feelings of helplessness.

Children who have been repeatedly hit often want to seek revenge. Getting back is a common result of spanking. Young children who can't hit back may seek revenge in other ways, such as breaking something that belongs to the parents, writing on the walls, or stealing. Studies have generally shown that the most punished children tend to be the most aggressive. They have learned that hitting is the way to deal with anger and frustration.

In years of research conducted by this writer in assessing the parenting and child rearing attitudes of thousands of teenagers and adults, it was establish that a remarkable transmission of attitudes is passed on from parents to children.

Utilizing the *Adult Adolescent Parenting Inventory (AAPI)*, attitudes regarding four specific parenting behaviors were assessed:

- Expectations parents have for children
- An ability to be empathic to the needs of children
- The belief in the use of corporal punishment as a means of discipline
- The definition of family roles

Not surprisingly, adolescents who had been repeatedly spanked and who were identified as abused had grossly inappropriate developmental expectations of children; lacked an empathic awareness of children's' needs; believe strongly in the use of corporal punishment as a means of disciplining children; and were confused about family roles, expressing reversals between parents and children. The tragedy of these findings is that these attitudes were similar to the attitudes of known adult child abusers.

These findings have been validated throughout the country in a number of settings. Children who have been repeatedly spanked develop views about parenting and child rearing that, if not replaced with more nurturing attitudes, may lead to abusive parenting and child rearing attitudes.

INSTEAD OF PUNISHMENT—DISCIPLINE

✓ *Express your feelings strongly—without attacking character.*

I'm furious that my new tool was left outside to rust in the rain!"

✓ *State your expectations.*

"I expect my tools to be returned after they've been borrowed."

✓ *Show the child how to make amends.*

"What this tool needs now is a little steel wool and a lot of elbow grease."

✓ *Give the child a choice.*

"You can borrow my tools and return them or you can give up the privilege of using them. You decide."

✓ *Take action.*

Lock the toolbox.

✓ *Problem solve.*

o "What can we work out so that you can use my tools when you need them and so that I'll be sure they're there when I need them?"

POSITIVE DISCIPLINE

There is no magic formula for discipline, no tried and true method that works in every situation. There are always at least several helpful methods that will be effective, depending on the child's mood, our own, and what's happening at the moment. Once we commit ourselves to using the positive methods and practice them daily, they become second nature. Here are some to try:

✓ Don't assume a child knows your rules. Make expectations clear.
✓ Redirect. "The chair isn't for jumping on. Jump on that mat."
✓ Be encouraging. "I know you can put the toys away on time." This gets cooperation, whereas a negative remark, "You never get your jobs done," brings more misbehavior.
✓ Involve children in decisions. Ask them to help think of a solution to the problem.
✓ Give choice, "Play indoors with the quiet toy or outside with the ball." Children are more agreeable when they've some say.
✓ Sometimes, there is no choice: "You'd like to stay up later, but 8:00 o'clock is your bedtime."
✓ Use humor. It lightens everyone's mood. "Abra-ka-dabra and your pajamas are on."
✓ Have a child take responsibility. If he has hurt his sister's feelings, ask him to think of a way to make her feel better.
✓ Appreciate good behavior and notice improvements. Your praise is the child's incentive to keep it up!

***When words aren't winning a child's cooperation,
do not take a punitive stance.
Turn to helpful actions:***

✓ Remove any object or game the child is misusing until she's ready to use it correctly.
✓ Remove a privilege that's being misused. But as soon as the child is ready to handle it responsibly, return the privilege. This shows you're on the child's side. When he's capable of behaving correctly, you're glad of it.

When we set limits in a positive way, we help children to grow in a nurturing, supportive environment. We eliminate children's fear of adults, and put trust in its place.

APPROACHES TO DISCIPLINE

Most of us automatically use the methods of discipline that we are most familiar with—what our parents used to discipline us.

However, discipline is taught in several ways:

- Setting an example by your own behavior
- Allowing a child to make mistakes and helping him/her to recover
- Letting the child know that you have positive expectations for him/her which she can realistically meet
- Teaching him/her about cause and effect
- Helping him/her to live and work in a group
- Emphasizing with him/her the things she has done right as well

HINTS:

Prevention
Love abundantly
Discipline constructively
Be consistent
Be clear
Administer in private
Be reasonable and understanding
Be flexible
Discourage continued dependency
Be authoritative
Spend time together
Really listen
Develop mutual respect
Be realistic

RULES FOR CORRECTIVE MEASURE:

- ✓ Relate the consequence to the offense
- ✓ Make consequences by psychologically correct for the child
- ✓ Remember, no corporal punishment
- ✓ Give logical reasons for the consequences
- ✓ Admit your mistakes
- ✓ Do not take remedial action when you are angry
- ✓ Be truthful
- ✓ Try to find out the underlying causes—all behavior has meaning
- ✓ Do not expect him/her to tell you why she did something
- ✓ Be encouraging and praising
- ✓ Remember, all feelings are acceptable
- ✓ Try to say "yes"
- ✓ Be disciplined yourself

APPROACHES TO DISCIPLINE

TECHNIQUES FOR PRE-TEENS

Realistic Expectations:

✓ Behavior may mimic adolescence.
✓ Girls may be more mature in their thinking and in their concerns than boys.
✓ Both boys and girls may be moody and involved with the expression of feelings.
✓ The preteen exhibits the growth of abstract logic, but is not consistent with it.
✓ The preteen may exhibit beginning attempts to break away.
✓ A sense of ethics should be well developed.
✓ Peer pressure may be more potent that loyalty to the family.

Parental Goals:

✓ Make sure your child has had a substantial education in sexual matters.
✓ Develop negotiating skills.
✓ Help your child develop good judgment and civic responsibility.
✓ Protect your child's physical and emotional health.

Techniques:

• Handle sensitive matters delicately. Try to avoid very harsh punishments and empty threats.
• Provide clear guidelines for sexual and social conduct.
• Be a model for restraint and civilization.
• Provide ample education regarding dangers of drugs, alcohol and smoking.
• Give your child handy excuses to withstand peer pressure so he can avoid drugs, alcohol and smoking.

- Give your child opportunities for making judgments.
- Make it clear that you will not condone cheating, lying, stealing, vandalism, rude and fresh behavior or the taking of drugs, alcohol, or tobacco.
- Allow your child to experience logically related punishments; if those are impossible, them make it clear that privileges will be removed or the child will be grounded for infractions.
- Make limits clear.
- Take your child's opinions seriously. Do not patronize a competing viewpoint.

POINTS TO REMEMBER:

1. **Effective discipline helps children learn self-control and cooperation.**
2. **Reward and punishment are not effective methods of discipline.** They teach children to expect an adult to be responsible for their behavior.
3. In selecting an appropriate method, it's important to **consider a child's developmental level.**
4. **Effective methods of discipline are:**

   - Distracting the child
   - Ignoring misbehavior when appropriate
   - Structuring the environment
   - Controlling the situation, not the child
   - Involving the child through choices and consequences
   - Planning time for loving
   - Letting go
   - Increasing your consistency
   - Noticing positive behavior
   - Excluding the child with a time out

5. **Use natural and logical consequences to give choices to a child.** Natural consequences result from going against the laws

of nature. Logical consequences are the result of going against the rules of social cooperation.

6. **Logical consequences**

- Express the rules of social living
- Are related to the misbehavior
- Separate the deed from the doer
- Are concerned with what will happen now, not with past behavior
- Are given in a friendly way
- Permit choice

GUIDELINES FOR USING LOGICAL CONSEQUENCES:

- When a child makes a decision, let the decision stand—for the moment. Later give the child another opportunity to cooperate.
- Increase the amount of time for the consequences each time the same misbehavior happens.
- When you give a child a choice, phrase the choice respectfully.
- Respect the child's choice.
- Say as little as possible and avoid nagging or threatening.
- Make it clear when there is no choice.
- Keep hostility out of consequences.
- Spending some quality time each day with your child is good for your relationship and can help prevent behavior problems.
- Too much protection, permissiveness, or demands for obedience will prevent children from becoming independent.
- A time-out is a form of logical consequences. Use it as a last resort, when other methods haven't worked.
- Choose a relaxed time to teach skills and make the training fun.

TAKE A MOMENT TO LISTEN

Denis Waithy
From *Seeds of Greatness*

Take a moment to listen today
To what your children are trying to say'
Listen today, whatever you do,
Or they won't be there to listen to you.
Listen to their problems. Listen for their needs.
Praise their smallest triumphs.
Praise their smallest deeds.
Tolerate their chatter. Amplify their laughter.

MODULE 11

Building Your Child's Self Esttem and
Developing Encouragement Skills

CONSTRUCTIVE CRITICISM
BUILDING SELF ESTEEM?

Building your child's self-esteem and feelings of worth is something all parents want for their children. Even though we all want the best for our children and have good intentions, our methods fall short of desired results.

In the following statements, consider the difference between our ideals and what we actually do. Try to think of actions that would be more consistent with the ideals.

Our ideal	What we really do
My child should be responsible and independent.	Force child to perform; do child's work for them.
My child should be respectful and courteous.	Talk down to the child; criticize, distrust, lecture, and punish child.
My child should be happy.	Compliment success, but dwell on mistakes; tell child she can do better.
My child should feel adequate, be courageous, and feel good about him herself.	Do too much for child, implying child is not capable; criticize, make fun of, refuse to allow child to try difficult tasks.

Often our day-to-day relationships with our children do not match our honorable intentions and ideals—and there is a reason for this. Our society has influenced us to be expert at finding fault, to expect the worst, and, in general, to be discouraging toward our children and ourselves.

> **We do not have to perpetuate this discouraging cycle.**

"I've got two A's," the small boy cried.
His voice was filled with glee.
His father very bluntly asked,
"Why didn't you get three?"
"Mom, I've got the dishes done,"
The girl called from the door.
Her mother very calmly said,
"And did you sweep the floor?"
"I've mowed the grass," the tall boy said,
"And put the mower away."
His father asked him with a shrug,
"Did you remember to clean off the clay?"
The children in the house next door,
Seemed happy and content.
The same things happened over there,
But this is how it went.
"I've got two A's," the small boy cried.
His voice was filled with glee.
His father proudly said, "That's great!
I'm glad you live with me!"
"Mom, I've got the dishes done,"
The girl called from the door.
Her mother smiled and softly said,
"Each day I love you more."
I've mowed the grass," the tall boy said,
"And put the mower away."
His father answered with great joy,
"Son, you've made my day."
Children deserve a little praise,
For tasks they're asked to do.
If they're to lead a happy life,
So much depends on you.

Dr. Joan D. Atwood

ATTITUDES AND BEHAVIORS TO ELIMINATE

- **Negative Expectations**: Children internalize the expectations of adults, i.e., when we believe a child won't succeed at a difficult task, we communicate that belief in one-way or another.
- **Unreasonably High Standards**: We communicate that we expect them to do better, and let them know that whatever they do, it's never as good as it could have been.
- **Promoting Competition between Brothers and Sisters**: We praise the successful child while we ignore or criticize the unsuccessful child. Comparisons may be expressed non-verbally: a gesture or a facial expression can trigger competition as effectively as a comment.
- **Over-ambition**: This attitude may influence children not to try anything unless they are certain they will be tops, with the result that they avoid areas in which they see possible failure.
- **Double Standards**: Children recognize that certain socially prescribed rights and privileges, such as driving a car, are restricted to age. But, when parents assume other rights and privileges and deny them to children, this tells the children that they are of less value in the family.

ATTITUDES AND BEHAVIORS THAT ENCOURAGE

- **Accept your Children as They Are, Not Only as They Could Be**: If we want our children to see themselves as worthwhile persons, we must genuinely accept them as they are, with all their imperfections.
- **Ignore Tattling**: Paying attention to tattling has a very discouraging effect. Children use tattling to make themselves look good or to get even.
- **Be Positive**: An encouraging parent stops using negative comments about a child. When problems arise, the encouraging parent uses methods that are based on respect for the

child—listening, I-messages, problem-solving, and natural and logical consequences.

- **Recognize Effort and Improvement As well As Final Accomplishment**: When parents hold out for achievement—a better grade in math, a neat room at home, some children conclude they are not good enough unless they approximate perfection.

- **Encourage Rather Than Praise**: At first glance, praise and encouragement appear to be the same process. The distinction is that praise is a type of reward and is based on competition. Encouragement, however, is given for effort or improvement. It focuses on the child's assets and strengths as a means for him/her to contribute to the good of all.

SEVEN STEPS TO FACILITATE POSITIVE CRITICISM

How do you give your child feedback without sounding mean or nasty? How do you tell them how to improve without them getting defensive or angry? Here are seven easy steps to facilitate positive criticism.

1. Describe what you see the problem to be without attacking the child, judging or moralizing. This will start the conversation without getting off to a discouraging start.
2. Make your feedback as specific as possible. Clear directions focused on the issue not the child. Remember: undesirable behaviors or grades are not the same as undesirable children.
3. Give feedback when the child is most ready to hear it. Find a time when there are few distractions, or when other activities will not have to be sacrificed, unless immediate attention is appropriate.
4. Check to see if your child understands what you are saying. Ask them to repeat or put it in their own words to see if it makes sense to them. They may feel your feedback is a personal attack. For example, asking them to perform a task a certain way may be interpreted as "You hate the way I do things!" Be sure to remain calm, repeat and then reassure them of what you said and intended to mean.
5. Give feedback in small doses, avoid overwhelming your child. This will facilitate participation and cooperation.
6. Use "I" statements and focus on how you think and feel to prevent defensive reactions.
7. If your child feels you are being mean or unreasonable, ask a neutral person

HOW TO ENCOURAGE DEVELOPMENT
OF HEALTHY SELF-ESTEEM

✓ Encourage good communication
✓ Use "I" messages

✓ Supply parental warmth, love, unconditional acceptance
✓ Have realistic expectations.
✓ Give encouragement
✓ Set definite limits on acceptable behavior.
✓ Respect the child.
✓ Teach decision-making skills
✓ Be a positive role model
✓ Place trust and give responsibility
✓ Be aware of strengths and assets
✓ Self-praise

Dr. Joan D. Atwood

101 WAYS TO PRAISE A CHILD

* Wow * Way To Go * Super * You're Special * Outstanding * Excellent
* Great * Good * Neat * Well Done * Remarkable * I Knew You
Could Do It * I'm Proud Of You * Fantastic * Super Star * Nice Work
* Looking Good * You're On Top Of It * Beautiful * Now You're
Flying * You're Catching On * Now You've Got It * You're Incredible
* Bravo * You're Fantastic * Hurray For You * You're On Target *
You're On Your Way * How Nice * How Smart * Good Job * That's
Incredible * Hot Dog * Dynamite * You're Beautiful * You're Unique
* Nothing Can Stop You Now * Good For You * I like You * You're
A Winner * Remarkable Job * Beautiful Work * Spectacular * You're
Spectacular * You're A Darling * You're Precious * Great Discovery *
You've Discovered The Secret * You Figured It Out * Fantastic Job *
Hip, Hip, Hurray * Bingo * Magnificent * Marvelous * Terrific * You're
Important * Phenomenal * You're Sensational * Super Work * Creative
Job * Super Job * Fantastic Job * Exceptional Performance * You're A
Real Trooper * You Are Responsible * You Are Exciting * You Learned
It Right * What An Imagination * What A Good Listener * You Are
Fun * You're Growing Up * You Tried Hard * You Care * Beautiful
Sharing * Outstanding Performance * You're A Good Friend * I Trust
You * You're Important * You Mean A Lot To Me * You Make Me
Happy * You Belong * You've Got A Friend * You Make Me Laugh *
You Brighten My Day * I Respect You * You Mean The World To Me *
That's Correct * You're A Joy * You're A Treasure * You're Wonderful *
You're Perfect * Awesome * A+ Plus Job * You're The Best * A Big Hug
* A Big Kiss * Say I Love You!

P.S. Remember, a smile is worth a thousand words.

POINTS TO REMEMBER

ENCOURAGEMENT

BUILDING YOUR CHILD'S CONFIDENCE AND FEELINGS OF WORTH

- Encouragement is the process of focusing on your children's assets and strengths in order to build their self-confidence and feelings of worth.
- Focus on what is good about the child or the situation. See the positive.
- Accept your children as they are. Don't make your love and acceptance dependent on their behavior.
- Have faith in your children so they can come to believe in themselves.
- Let your children know their worth. Recognize improvement and effort, not just accomplishment.
- Respect your children. It will lay the foundation of their self-respect.
- Praise is reserved for things well done. It implies a spirit of competition. Encouragement is given for effort or improvement. It implies a spirit of cooperation.
- The most powerful forces in human relationships are expectations. We can influence a person's behavior by changing our expectations of the person.
- Lack of faith in children helps them to anticipate failure.
- Standards that are too high invite failure and discouragement.
- Avoid subtle encouragement of competition between brothers and sisters.
- Avoid using discouraging words and actions.

- Avoid tacking qualifiers onto your words of encouragement. Don't "give with one hand and take away with the other."
- The sounds of encouragement are words that build feelings of adequacy...

> "I like the way you handled that."
> "I know you can handle it."
> "I appreciate what you did."
> "It looks as if you worked very hard on that."

MODULE 12

Closing Summaries

INVENTORY OF POSITIVE TRAITS
AND EXPERIENCES

What was the happiest period of your life?

_____

_____

_____

_____

_____

_____

_____

_____

What things do you do well?

_____

_____

_____

_____

_____

_____

_____

Tell me about a positive turning point in your life.

_____

_____

_____

_____

_____

_____

_____

Was there any time when you exhibited great courage? If yes, tell me about it.

_____

_____

_____

_____

_____

_____

_____

_____

What are some improvements you have made in yourself since beginning module me?

_____

_____

_____

_____

_____

_____

_____

Tell me about some (non-drug related) peak experiences you have had. You currently have. You would like to have.

_____

_____

_____

_____

_____

_____

_____

What are some things you want to do right now at this point in your life?

_____

_____

_____

_____

_____

_____

_____

_____

What does your family usually do on Thanksgiving?

_____

_____

_____

_____

_____

_____

_____

_____

What do they usually do at Christmas, Chanukah, etc.?

_____

_____

_____

_____

_____

_____

_____

_____

What books have you read recently that you liked?

_____

_____

_____

_____

_____

_____

_____

_____

How do you plan to get involved with your Mother/Father in their old age if they are still alive?

_____

_____

_____

_____

_____

_____

_____

_____

What are your favorite sports?

_____

_____

_____

_____

_____

_____

_____

_____

Do you have a hobby that you enjoy?

_____
_____
_____
_____
_____
_____
_____
_____
_____

What do your friends like about you?

_____
_____
_____
_____
_____
_____
_____
_____

What do your parents like about you?

_____
_____
_____
_____
_____
_____
_____
_____

What do your siblings like about you?

_____

_____

_____

_____

_____

_____

_____

_____

What are some things you really like about you?

_____

_____

_____

_____

_____

_____

_____

_____

What are some things you really believe in?

_____

_____

_____

_____

_____

_____

_____

_____

Where do you see yourself five years from now?

_____

_____

_____

_____

_____

_____

_____

_____

What are some ideas you have of the good life?

_____

_____

_____

_____

_____

_____

_____

_____

Is there anything you would like to change about yourself? What?

_____

_____

_____

_____

_____

_____

_____

_____

Tell me some of the things you feel and do that make you satisfied with your life.

_____

_____

_____

_____

_____

_____

_____

_____

_____

What are some of the things that you do that you are proud of?

_____

_____

_____

_____

_____

_____

_____

_____

What are some of the things you are really good at?

_____

_____

_____

_____

_____

_____

Describe something nice you have done for a person recently.

_____
_____
_____
_____
_____
_____
_____
_____
_____

What is the best thing you have done for someone else?

_____
_____
_____
_____
_____
_____
_____
_____

What is the best thing you have done for yourself?

_____
_____
_____
_____
_____
_____
_____
_____

What have you learned about yourself from taking this personal inventory?

_____

_____

_____

_____

_____

_____

_____

Tell me about the new you.

_____

_____

_____

_____

_____

_____

_____

Draw a picture of the new you.

EVALUATION OF THE WORKBOOK

1. What did you like the most about the workbook?

_____

_____

_____

_____

_____

_____

_____

_____

2. What didn't you like about the workbook?

_____

_____

_____

_____

_____

_____

_____

3. What is the most valuable lesson you learned?

_____

_____

_____

_____

_____

_____

_____

4. What changes have you seen in yourself?

_____

_____

_____

_____

_____

_____

_____

_____

5. What other topics would you have liked to learn more about?

_____

_____

_____

_____

_____

_____

_____

6. Did you learn anything interesting about yourself that you did not learn before?

_____

_____

_____

_____

_____

_____

_____

7. Do you think you have the skills to better control your anger and your stress?

_____

_____

_____

_____

_____

_____

_____

_____

Closing Exercises and Graduation

In this section you can review your anger control plans and rate the treatment components for their usefulness and familiarity. You will also complete a closing exercise and be awarded a certificate of completion.

Closing Exercise:

1. What have you learned from the parent education course?

_____

_____

_____

_____

_____

_____

_____

_____

_____

2. Thinking of all the information you learned while in this program, what strategies do you think will help you the most in terms of managing your anger?

_____

_____

_____

_____

_____

_____

_____

_____

_____

3. In what ways can you continue to improve your parenting skills? Do
   you feel there are any areas that still need improvement?

_____

_____

_____

_____

_____

_____

_____

_____

_____

NOTES

ADDITIONAL MATERIALS

Individual Intake Form

Date: _____

Name: _____

Address:_____City:_____Zip _____

Home Phone: _____ Cell Phone: _____

Email: _____

Referred by: _____

Occupation: _____ Place of Business _____

Work Address: _____

Work Phone: _____ Birth date: _____Age:____ Sex: _____

Is there any other person living in your household: _____ yes _____no

If yes, please give their names and their relationship to you _____
_____
_____
_____
_____

Have you ever been married? _____yes _____no

If yes, to whom and for how long?
_____

Do you have any children? _____yes _____no if yes, please list below:
_____

Counseling History

From: _____ to: _____ with Whom? _____

For What?

_____

_____

Basic Health: _____ good _____ fair _____ poor
When was your last physical exam?

_____

Who is your Physician? _____

Are you taking any medication at this time? _____ yes _____ no If yes, what?

_____

Are you taking any over the counter medications, herbs, supplements, etc.? ____ yes _____ no If yes, what?

_____

Are you taking any medications for allergies? _____ yes _____ no If yes, what?

_____

Do you have any physical, emotional, or mental condition now or in the past that I need to be aware of? _____yes _____no If yes, what?

_____

Have you ever been hospitalized? _____ yes _____ no if so, for what?

_____

CURRENT REASON FOR SEEKING COUNSELING:

Briefly describe the problem for which you wish to have counseling?

_____

_____

_____

What would you like to see happen as a result of counseling?

_____

_____

_____

The thing which concerns me the most right now is?

_____

_____

_____

IT IS CUSTOMARY TO PAY YOUR THERAPIST AFTER EACH SESSION.

A COUNSELING SESSION IS NORMALLY 50 MINUTES.

POLICY

A 24-HOUR CANCELLATION NOTICE IS APPRECIATED; OTHERWISE USUAL FEE WILL BE CHARGED.

I UNDERSTAND THAT SUICIDAL THREATS, HOMICIDAL THREATS OR CHILD ABUSE BY AN ADULT TO A CHILD WILL BE REPORTED.

I UNDERSTAND AND GIVE PERMISSION TO MY THERAPIST TO SEEK CLINICAL SUPERVISION OR CONSULTATION ABOUT MY SITUATION WHEN NECESSARY.

Signature: _____

Please print name: _____

Date: _____

DUTY TO WARN

Although confidentiality and privileged communication remain rights of all clients of psychotherapists according to state law, some courts have held that if an individual intends to take harmful or dangerous action against another human being, or against himself or herself, it is the psychotherapist's duty to warn the person or the family of the person who is likely to suffer the results himself or herself.

State Laws require that all mental health professionals report incidents of any type of child abuse or neglect to appropriate agencies.

The psychotherapist will under no circumstances inform such individuals without first sharing that intention with the client. Every effort will be made to resolve the issue before such a breach of confidentiality takes place.

_____   _____

Therapist's signature   Client's Signature

No Violence Contract

Physical violence is extremely harmful to all relationships. Participation in physically aggressive behavior on the part of one or both partners results in numerous negative consequences. Some of these effects include: loss of trust, loss of respect for self and partner, emotional and physical pain, lack of intimacy, and less time spent together. Interpersonal violence greatly interferes with progress in couple therapy. In fact, interpersonal violence and couple therapy are not compatible. For these reasons, we are making a commitment, both written and verbal, to stop all violence in our relationship.

By violence, we mean harming or threatening to harm your partner either physically (e.g., pushing, shoving, restraining) or emotionally (e.g., belittling, name calling).

We can tell that we are coming close to becoming violent when…

_____

_____

_____

To help prevent violence from occurring, we will do one or more of the following to stop ourselves from escalating when we begin to see the cues listed above:

_____

_____

_____

If any of the above items occur even once, we have decided that it would be best to discontinue relationship therapy and begin individual therapy until we are able to control our physical aggression toward each other.

_____   _____

Client's signature   Date

_____   _____

Client's signature   Date

_____   _____

Therapist's signature   Date

General References

APA, Controlling Anger -- Before It Controls You, http:www.apa. orgtopicscontrolanger.html

Barkley, R.A. (1997). *Defiant Children: A Clinician's Manual for Assessment and Parent Training.* 2nd Ed. New York: Guilford Press.

Beck, R. and Fernandez, E. (1998). Cognitive behavioral therapy in the treatment of anger: A meta-analysis. *Cognitive Therapy and Research,* 22, 63 – 74.

Butler, G. and Hope, T. (2007) *Managing Your Mind: The Mental Fitness Guide,* 2nd Ed. New York: Oxford University Press.

Chapman, R.A.; Shedlack, K.J.; and France, J. (2006). Stop, think, and relax: An adaptive self-control training strategy for individuals with mental retardation and coexisting psychiatric illness. *Cognitive and Behavioral Practice,* 13(3), 205 – 214.

Ellis, A. (1979). Rational-emotive therapy. In: Corsini, R. (Ed.), *Current Psychotherapies* (pp. 185 – 229). Itasca, II: Peacock Publishers.

Ellis, A. (1992). Anger: How to Live With and Without It, New York: Citadel Press Book.

Falcon, C. T. (2004). Controlling Anger in Relationships, http:www. sensiblepsychology.comimproving_anger.htm

Feindler, E.L. (2006). *Anger Related Disorders: A Practitioner's Guide to Comparative Treatments* (Ed.). New York: Springer Publishing Co.

Gentry, D.W. (2000). Anger-Free: Ten Basic Steps to Managing Your Anger, Morrow, William & Co.

Gorkin, M. (081700). "ALARMING "YOU"S or DISARMING "I"S: POWER STRUGGLES vs. POWERFUL STRATEGIES PART I", http:www.selfhelpmagazine.comarticlesgrowthaggression.html

Gorkin, M. (1986) "Anger or Aggression: Confronting the Passionate Edge," Legal Assistant Today

Gorkin, M. (081700). "ALARMING "YOU"S or DISARMING "I"S: POWER STRUGGLES vs. POWERFUL STRATEGIES PART I", http:www.selfhelpmagazine.comarticlesgrowthaggression.html
Hankins, G. and Hankins, C. (1988). Prescription for Anger, New York: Warner.

Granath, J.; Ingvarsson, S.; and von Thiele, U. (2006). Stress management: A randomized study of cognitive behavior therapy and yoga. *Cognitive Behavior Therapy*, 35(1), 3 – 10.

Heimberg, R.G., and Juster, H.R. (1994). Treatment of social phobia in cognitive behavioral groups. *Journal of Clinical Psychology*, 55, 38 – 46.

Hoyt, M.F. (1993). Group therapy in an HMO. *HMO Practice*, 7, 127 – 132.

Lerner, H.G. (2000). The Dance of Anger: A Woman's Guide to Changing the Patterns of Intimate Relationships, Harper Trade

Luhn, R. R. (1992) Managing Anger, Menlo Park, Cal.: Crisp Publications.

McKenzie, C. (052898). "Anger what is it? And why – plus self-test", http:www.performance-appraisals.orgcgi-binlinksjump.cgi?ID=1702

Phillips, L.H.; Henry, J.D.; and Hosie, J.A. (2006). Age, anger regulation and well-being. *Aging & Mental Health*, 10(3), 250 – 256.

Potter-Efron, R. (2005). *Handbook of Anger Management: Individual, Couple, Family, and Group Approaches*. New York: Hawthorn Press, Inc.

Reilly, P.M., and Gruszski, R. (1984). A structured didactic model for men for controlling family violence. *International Journal of Offender Therapy and Comparative Criminology*, 28, 223 – 235.

Robertson, K. and Murachver, T. (2007). It takes two to tangles: Gender symmetry in intimate partner violence. *Basic and Applied Social Psychology*, 29(2), 109 –118.

Straus, M; Gelles, R.; and Steinmetz, S. (1980). *Behind Closed Doors: Violence in the American Family*. Garden City, NY: Doubleday.

Tower, L.E. (2007). Group work with a new population: Women in domestic relationships responding to violence with violence. *Women and Therapy*, 30(1-2), 35 – 60.

Walker, L. (1979). *The Battered Woman*. New York: Harper & Row.

Yalom, I.D. (1995). *The Theory and Practice of Group Psychotherapy*. 4th Ed. New York: Basic Books, Inc.

The Case of Anthony. Feindler, Eva L.; *In: Anger* related disorders: A practitioner's guide to comparative treatments. Feindler, Eva L.; New York, NY, US: Springer Publishing Co, 2006. pp. 29-42. [Chapter]

Review of Anger management: The complete treatment guidebook for practitioners. Smith, Kent; ANZJFT Australian and New Zealand Journal of Family Therapy, Vol 27(1), Mar 2006. pp. 56-57. [Review-Book]

Gender-specific symptoms of depression and anger attacks. Winkler, Dietmar; Pjrek, Edda; Kasper, Siegfried; Journal of Men's Health & Gender, Vol 3(1), Mar 2006. pp. 19-24. [Journal Article]

Review of Psychoanalysis, Violence and Rage-Type Murder. Asser, Jonathan; Psychodynamic Practice: Individuals, Groups and Organizations, Vol 12(1), Feb 2006. pp. 119-121. [Review-Book]

References for Groups

Charrier, G.O. (1974). Cog's ladder: A model of group development. In J.W. Pfeiffer & J.E. Jones (Eds.), the 1974 annual handbook for group facilitators. San Diego, CA: Pfeiffer & Company.

Cooke, P., & Widdis, W. (1988). Guidelines for interventions in groups. Unpublished manuscript.

Tuckman, B.W., & Jensen, M.A.C. (1977, December) Stages of small group development revisited. Group organization Studies, 2(4), 419427.

References for Emotional Intelligence

Antonakis, J. (2003). Why 'emotional intelligence' does not predict leadership effectiveness: A comment on Prati, Douglas, Ferris, Ameter, and Buckley. *The International Journal of Organizational Analysis, 11(4), 355-361.*

Antonakis, J. (2004). On why "emotional intelligence" will not predict leadership effectiveness beyond IQ or the "big five": An extension and rejoinder. Organizational Analysis, 12(2), 171-182.

Beasley, K. (1987, May) *the Emotional Quotient.* Mensa Magazine: United Kingdom Edition.

Bradberry, Travis. And Greaves, Jean. (2005). "The Emotional Intelligence Quickbook", New York: Simon and Schuster.

Bradberry, Travis and Greaves, Jean. "Hearless Bosses?" *Harvard Business Review*, December 1, 2005.

Bradberry, Travis. (2007). "The Personality Code," New York: Putnam

Ciarrochi, H. and Mayer, J. (2005). "Can Self-Report Measures Contribute to the Study of Emotional Intelligence? A Conversation between Joseph Ciarrochi and John D. Mayer" accessed January 2, 2006.

Darwin, C., 1872. Origin of Species, Sixth Edition. Senate, London.

Eysenck, H. (2000). *Intelligence: A New Look*, Transaction Publishers, (ISBN 0-7658-0707-6), pp. 109-110.

Fisher, Roger, and Shapiro, Daniel. (2005). *Beyond Reason: Using Emotions as You Negotiate. New York: Viking Penguin.*

Freedman, J. (2007). *At the heart of leadership.* California: Six Seconds.

Gardner, H. (1975) *The Shattered Mind.* New York: Knopf.

Gibbs, Nancy (1995, October 2). The EQ Factor. *Time Magazine.* Web reference at http:www.time.comtimeclassroompsychunit5_article1.html accessed January 2, 2006.

Goleman, D. (1996). *Emotional Intelligence: why it can matter more than IQ.* London: Bloomsbury. (ISBN 0-7475-2622-2)MacCann, C., Roberts, R.D., Matthews, G., & Zeidner, M. (2004). Consensus scoring and empirical option weighting of performance-based emotional intelligence tests. *Personality & Individual Differences, 36,* 645-662.

Mayer, J. (2005a). "Can Emotional Knowledge be improved? Can you raise emotional intelligence?" The University of New Hampshire. Web reference at http:www.unh.eduemotional_intelligenceei%20 Improveei%20Rasing%20EI.htmaccessed January 2, 2006.

Mayer, J. (2005b) "Emotional Intelligence Information: A Site Dedicated to Communicating Scientific Information about Emotional Intelligence, Including Relevant Aspects of Emotions, Cognition, and Personality." The University of New Hampshire. Web reference at http:www.unh. eduemotional_intelligenceindex.html accessed January 2, 2006.

Mayer, J. (2005c). "Is EI the Best Predictor of Success in Life?" The University of New Hampshire. Web reference at http:www.unh. eduemotional_intelligenceei%20Controversieseicontroversy1%20 best%20predictor.htm accessed January 2, 2006.

Mayer, J. (2005c). "How Do You Measure Emotional Intelligence?" The University of New Hampshire. Web reference at [1] accessed January 2, 2006.

Mayer, J.D. & Salovey, P. (1993). The intelligence of emotional intelligence. *Intelligence*, 17, 433-442.

Mayer, J., Salovey, P., Caruso, D.R., and Sitarenios, G. (2001) "Emotional intelligence as a standard intelligence." *Emotion*, 1, 232-242.

Payne, W.L. (1985). A study of emotion: developing emotional intelligence; self-integration; relating to fear, pain and desire (theory, structure of reality, problem-solving, contraction expansion, tuning incoming out letting go). A Doctoral Dissertation. Cincinnati, OH: The Union for Experimenting Colleges and Universities (now the Union Institute). Abstract available at http:eqi.orgpayne.htm

Roberts, R.D., Zeidner, M., and Matthews, G. (2001). Does emotional intelligence meet traditional standards for an intelligence? Some new data and conclusions. *Emotion, 1*, p. 196-231. Web pre-publication version available at http:eqi.orgei_abs4.htm accessed 19 Sept 2006.

Salovey, P. & David S. (Ed.s). (1997). Emotional development and Emotional Intelligence: Educational implications. New York: Basic Books. (ISBN 978-0465095872)

Salovey, P. and Mayer, J.D. (1990). "Emotional intelligence." *Imagination, Cognition, and Personality*, 9(1990), 185-211. [2]

Schutte, N.S., Malouff, J.M., Hall, L.E., Haggerty, D.J., Cooper, J.T., Golden, C.J., & Dornheim, L. (1998). Development and validation of a measure of emotional intelligence. Personality and Individual Differences, 25, 167-177.

Smith, M. K. (2002) "Howard Gardner and multiple intelligences," *the encyclopedia of informal education*, Downloaded from http:www.infed. orgthinkersgardner.htm on October 31, 2005.

Stein, S and Book, H. "The EQ Edge". Toronto: Jossey-Bass.

Stein, S (1997). Men and Women Have Different Kinds and Levels of Emotional Intelligence, EQ for Both Sexes is Key to Workplace Success.

Technical Brochures regarding the psychometric properties of the BOEI (Benchmark of Emotional Intelligence), EQ-I, and MSCEIT.

Tett, R. P., Fox, K. E., & Wang, A. (2005). Development and validation of a self-report measure of emotional intelligence as a multidimensional trait domain. *Personality and Social Psychology Bulletin, 31*, 859-888.

Thorndike, R.K. (1920). "Intelligence and Its Uses," *Harper's Magazine* 140, 227-335.

Warneka, T. (2006). *Leading People the Black Belt Way: Conquering the Five Core Problems Facing Leaders Today*. Asogomi Press. Cleveland, Ohio.

Waterhouse, Lynn. (2006a). Multiple Intelligences, the Mozart Effect, and Emotional Intelligence: A critical review. Educational Psychologist, 41(4), Fall, pp. 207-225.

Waterhouse, Lynn. (2006b). "Inadequate Evidence for Multiple Intelligences, Mozart Effect, and Emotional Intelligence Theories." Educational Psychologist, 41(4), Fall, pp. 247-255.

Read more on Family Education: http:life.familyeducation.comconnecting-with-your-teenparentchild-relationships73209.html#ixzz2LYphYHhN

Read more on Family Education: http:life.familyeducation.comconnecting-with-your-teenparentchild-relationships73209.html#ixzz2LYpbD5za

Read more on Family Education: http:life.familyeducation.comconnecting-with-your-teenparentchild-relationships73209.html#ixzz2LYpWUYhD

Read more on Family Education: http:life.familyeducation.comconnecting-with-your-teenparentchild-relationships73209.html#ixzz2LYpRySjH

Read more on Family Education: http:life.familyeducation.comconnecting-with-your-teenparentchild-relationships73209.html#ixzz2LYpL952T

Read more on Family Education: http:life.familyeducation.comconnecting-with-your-teenparentchild-relationships73209.html#ixzz2LYpG1sL8

Read more on Family Education: http:life.familyeducation.comconnecting-with-your-teenparentchild-relationships73209.html#ixzz2LYp9BhHV

Read more on Family Education: http:life.familyeducation.comconnecting-with-your-teenparentchild-relationships73209.html#ixzz2LYp0TTd7

Read more on Family Education: http:life.familyeducation.comconnecting-with-your-teenparentchild-relationships73209.html#ixzz2LYouWPgQ

Read more on Family Education: http:life.familyeducation.comconnecting-with-your-teenparentchild-relationships73209.html#ixzz2LYolwmr4

Read more: http:www.empoweringparents.comfive-secrets-for-communicating-with-teenagers.php#ixzz2LYoOMph7

Elkind, D. 1994. *Parenting your teenager.* New York: Ballantine Books.

Patterson, G. R., and M. S. Forgatch. 1987. *Parents and adolescents living together, Part 1:* The basics. Eugene, OR: Castalia.

Forgatch, M. S., and G. R. Patterson. 1989. *Parents and adolescents living together, Part 2:* Family problem solving. Eugene, OR: Castalia.

Steinberg, L. D., and A. Levine. 1997. *You and your adolescent: a parent's guide for ages 10 to 20.* New York: Harper Collins Publisher.

Depression Cured at Last by Sherry Rogers, M.D.

Stop ADD Naturally by Billie J. Sahley, Ph.D.

Heal with Amino Acids by Billie J. Sahley, Ph.D. and Katherine Birkner, Ph.D.

Break Your Prescribed Addiction by Billie J. Sahley, Ph.D. and Katherine Birkner, Ph.D.

Read more on Family Education: http:life.familyeducation.comteenanger 39357.html#ixzz2LYk42Dgd

Read more: http:www.empoweringparents.comthe-angry-explosive-teen-what-you-should-and-should-not-do.php#ixzz2LYjb6NBx

Read more: http:www.empoweringparents.comthe-angry-explosive-teen-what-you-should-and-should-not-do.php#ixzz2LYjVkeTm

Printed in the United States
By Bookmasters